Elon Musk:

Moving the World One Technology at a Time

Elon Musk:

Moving the World One Technology at a Time

Insight and Analysis into the Life and Accomplishments of a Technology Mogul

JR MacGregor

Elon Musk: Moving the World One Technology at a Time

Insight and Analysis into the Life and Accomplishments of a Technology Mogul

Published by CAC Publishing LLC.

ISBN 978-1-948489-44-7 paperback

ISBN 978-1-948489-42-3 eBook

This book is dedicated to those innovators that dream of one day changing the world for the better. To those who are always a step ahead of their time and often misunderstood for it. Keep innovating, keep thinking, and never give up until you've accomplished the task.

Make sure to check out the first book in this 'Billionaire Visionaries' series:

Jeff Bezos: The Force Behind the Brand

Table of Contents

Chapter 1 An Overview

"When something is important enough, you do it even if the odds are not in your favor."
— Elon Musk

I am part of a generation, as is Musk, that grew up in a world where man has walked on the moon. Born shortly after the Apollo missions where all the jocks with the right stuff had launched the imagination of a planet. But that is the extent of our affinity to space travel – stories of the glory of histories past.

Therefore, there was always this thing in me that has seen our generation as lacking in the kind of tenacity that it takes to innovate big things – not just innovate social websites to share photos from the last family trip (which really, no one wants to see) and porn. These are all really wussy innovations – and by then it's been some time since we've had some really good kick-in-the-pants kind of innovation and collective reaching for the stars.

We haven't done much in a long time. Sure, we've got the Internet – but so what? Aside from shopping and posting pictures?

Then came the shuttle years when I was in high school. And since then there have been events here and there that didn't quite match up to Armstrong's first step, or Lovell's thirteen days of valor. Until this afternoon.

I hadn't planned on taking time off my already jammed schedule to watch what would be a frail attempt at a webcast of the Falcon Heavy being launched. The experience reminded me of the numerous live webcasts that were anxiety-ridden between the delayed telecasts, dropped transmissions, poor sound, grainy visuals and pressing matters that occupied the reality of my day. But against all intents to the contrary, I was late and checked my YouTube feed only to find that either I had the time wrong or the launch was delayed. Eventually, the live cast started with a couple of enthusiastic SpaceX employees and a whole bunch in the background. There was a vibe I had not recognized. It was invigorating, and I stayed.

The moments to the countdown moved at pace and as precisely as a Swiss watch – or should I say, with the precision of Musk. It was fairly flawless; the countdown started and the next thing I know spaceman was in his joyride pose in the Tesla convertible on his way to Mars. I was surprised, exhilarated, and full of appreciation for the steps that had been taken. Even if launching a car into space has got to be one of the most brilliant PR stunts ever concocted, planned, and executed, it was a testament to what we can do as individuals, as a team, and as a species.

But the thing that I thought was ironic was the fact that it was probably the world's only electric car to have used kerosene to get to its destination – and lots of it. It got me to think about the dichotomy of Musk's mind. On the one hand he is constantly talking about environmental issues and why we need to buy electric cars and use solar – all of which are spot on; but then, on the other hand, he lit a match to a kerosene rocket – the biggest one ever, and that will be the first of many. So, the dichotomy of his intentions and his mind are apparent. He swings from one state of existence into the next without effort, and you see it even in his views of AI. Or maybe it is just the way we humans advocate ideals but partake in necessities (even if the later does go against the former). Musk is no different decrying the ills of AI while using it in his products smacks of hypocrisy but, let's face it; human beings are complex. We tend to roll with the punches and we have different opinions on different things based on the circumstances that surround those events.

To the layperson who is not an adoring fan (disclosure – I am neither a fan who thinks he is the next Jobs, Edison or Tesla; nor am I totally aghast at his actions, words, and deeds) Musk comes off as a bit of a kooky character, from the way he looks to the way he speaks. I give him a pass on that, but I do want to make a lesson out of his life.

He is obviously aware that he comes off as a little crazy, and far be it for me to label him as such since I am not qualified in any way to make such proclamations – but the fact that he can ask others if they think he is crazy shows that he either believes it, someone has told him so, or he is holding on really tight. I don't begrudge him one way or the other because I strongly believe that, to change the world, you have to walk the fine line between mediocre and insane – every once in a while tipping over to the side of crazy. And that is what, with all due respect, Elon Musk is.

But I am not here to judge. We all have to balance our ideals because we live in the real world. But that just brings me back to the first point about Musk – the dichotomy of his mind. He sees things in two dimensions. And sometimes what you see in one dimension can be totally at odds with what you see in a different dimension. This is the point of departure we want to make with this book and the look that we take into the perceived motivations and life of this larger-than-life mountain mover.

I chose Elon as someone to write about because it's someone that each and every one of us can relate to and, if you decide to make it in life, no matter which corner of the world you come from – and this includes the corners of the world that go beyond just first world countries, but the ones where kids grow up surrounded by things that most of us can't even imagine. Musk grew up surrounded by Apartheid in South Africa, and that's not the most conducive places for kids – especially smart ones. It was also a place that was marinated and drenched with racism – with effects unlike what our typical views of racism look like. It was a whole different brand of racism that was mixed with ungodly and evil acts and outcomes. That sort of environment breeds contempt for all creation and creates a social environment that you can't imagine.

There are countless stories that you can easily Google about what life was like in Apartheid South Africa. Two great men – long before Musk was born – have sprung from the clutches of this past – India's Gandhi, and South Africa's Mandela. Both these men were in the midst of the atrocities and cruelties of a mindset that was based on the color of one's skin.

Let me just give you an idea of the mindset in South Africa before Musk was born and through the time he was there.

There were three classifications of race: European, Colored, and African. Whites were European (a term of social and legal privilege – not necessarily to be associated with the continent), of course, coloreds were those of mixed heritage and Africans were black. And they had tests for these classifications. These tests for race were as arbitrary as they could get. For instance, your race was determined by such things as the moons of your fingers. If they were off-white, then that meant you have Black blood and that resulted in your being either colored or out and out black. People from Chinese heritage were referred to as colored, yet those with Japanese ancestors were considered white. Go figure.

Caucasians were obviously white, and so referred to as Europeans – and if you were blonde and blue-eyed, all the better. There was another interesting, yet albeit random test, and that was the test of your hair. If they put a pencil in your hair and it rolled off then, even though you looked dark skinned, you could be considered colored – a promotion of sorts. On the other hand, if the pencils remained in your hair and didn't fall, then you have knotty nappy hair and that made you African.

By no measure, in any civilized world, can this be considered remotely amusing or innocuous. This was institutionalized and systemic racism of the vilest kind and, while this book is not about race politics in South Africa, it goes to show the mindset of people in the country that Elon Musk spent the early part of his life with.

In the cities, Africans (remember, that's the term for those with black skin) were not allowed access after dark, and there was one of two ways for them to be in the city. They needed to have permission and they needed to be placed in housing that was adjacent to the Whites that they worked for. The way it was known, if the African had permission to be in the city after dark, was that it would be stamped in their Passbook – something that all Africans (blacks), and only Africans, had to carry on their person at all times. Europeans had no such burden.

Violence against Africans was widespread. Europeans could abuse and mistreat Africans with impunity, and the bravado that was part of the collective mindset was prevalent. Long train rides were not safe – for anyone, much less road travel. These were the kinds of conditions that were daily realities for those who lived in South Africa. The narrative here and in the rest of the book really doesn't even come close to scratching the surface to the deplorable psychological stresses it places on a person, especially if that person is already empathic in nature and one who is not naturally given to illogical biases of race. Such was the basis of displeasure that Musk faced growing up.

Africans were not allowed to attend school, but coloreds were, so many people tried to change their race by doing the pencil test, and tens of thousands were successful. But the gang violence did not abate. There was an ingrained hatred of those of colored skin and there was a misunderstanding of the value of life among all. Even those who were colored or black in South Africa were convinced after some time of their place in the works. About thirty years ago, I was traveling with a teenager of colored classification. We rode to the city together from Heathrow Airport and, along the way, the city was going about its business, among which were garbage collectors putting trash bins by the side of trucks and emptying them in there. My new friend was in shock to see 'white men' do the work and he said that this can't be – it's not right. The notion in him that was ingrained so deeply was that it was unnatural for a man of white skin to do jobs of labor. It took a few years before he realized that all men were indeed created equal. But if he felt that way imagine how the white population of South Africa felt and how much of that dictated the way they behaved to the people around them. A sense of entitlement and a bullying sense of bravado. And even though Musk was neither colored nor African, he too felt the tip of the bravado's whip.

His experience during high school was more than just that of a school nerd getting trashed at the hand of the neighborhood bullies. It was a mix of personal animus they had for him and the typical bravado of a country that had trickled down to the youth of the city – and that was something that did not look at the equality between men, rather it was always White over Black, Strong over Meek, Brawn over Brains.

There was a stretch of time in high school when he was literally stuck between the devil and the deep blue sea. The only difference was that it wasn't a choice so much as a timeshare. He split his days between time at school where he attended classes, talked to friends, and either got beat up or spent the afternoon running and hiding from those who had marked him as quarry; then he packed up and went home for the second half of his day and there he would read, do his chores, read some more and deal with the difficulties of a father that was the cause of so much pain and anguish in his and his sibling's lives. More on that part of his life in the chapters to follow.

Then there is this third factor – National Service. Serving in the military during National Service is something every teenager does. A number of countries have this in place, although it is not something that we have here in the US. It's tantamount to a draft, but it is more of a compulsory perpetual thing where every person, by the time they reach a certain age, have to enlist and serve a mandatory period of time where they are trained and deployed if need be. This is supposed to serve two purposes. The first is that it is supposed to provide the country with able young men to take part in military duties, which include domestic control if need be. The second, and the reason it is so in many countries, is that it is meant to enhance the character and personalities of young men in the country. It has been proven that a two-year stint in the military increases the person's ability to succeed in the world at large and to be able to learn the necessary discipline to be part of a workforce that is effective.

This thing about having to join the military was not something that Musk was too keen on. In fact, he hated the idea of having to get into an isolated environment where he would be exposed to more bravado and the possibility of more ragging and bullying – probably something that would be worse than what he had faced in school. The second thing about joining the military, even if it was just for National Service, was that there was a lot of brainwashing going on in what they needed to do and the politics of Apartheid had a lot to do with that. He would have to be forced to listen to that propaganda – and what's worse, he would probably have to enforce it when deployed. The beating of blacks and the unnecessary abuse inflicted on them by the military was not a secret. If creating a life and advancing his interest in electronics and software were the 'pull' he felt in going to America, then the fear of joining the military was the 'push' to get out of Apartheid South Africa.

There are stories abound all across the internet – so many in fact that I was initially not planning to include it in this book. But no matter how much I tried to put it away, it is not entirely possible to give you an accurate picture of the man or the forces that shape a man – and in this case the forces that shaped Musk – without going into the brutal beating he took as a kid and the one that brought him within inches of his life.

The forces that existed around him as a child, from the break-up of a happy home to the violence he was treated with in the schoolyard on a daily basis, and the harsh environment of the paternal home after his parents' divorce would have been daunting for any other kid. Even if I had to go through that, I think that I would have found myself going crazy and, I suspect, Musk is also very cognizant about how he acts so that he does not come off as being crazy.

But when you add these events to the fact that he was subjected to some of the harshest conditions one could imagine, but yet he kept his intellectual ability intact, it shows the resilience of the human spirit. I define the ability that all of us possess, to varying degrees. It defines the cache of strength and mental ability that we can turn to when things get tough and when hope is hard to distinguish from pipe dreams.

It has always been my understanding, and all my books on famous figures in history and commerce reflect this, that biographies are not just about names, dates, places, and salacious fragments of information. Biographies are about how successful individuals made it great and made it beyond what we sometimes admire – and, let's be honest, sometimes loathe.

For biographies to make sense, we need to see them in context and we need to look at the content with understanding instead of judgment. When you judge a person, the lessons they have to offer are wasted. Everyone has lessons to teach us. Churchill or Hitler, Gandhi or Lenin, the lessons in life and the path to our personal growth are there if we just look without judgment and malice. The same goes for the likes of Gates, Jobs, and Branson – all of whom I've written about, and it certainly goes with Musk.

The reason I decided to write about Musk is not because of the wealth he has managed to amass – I certainly don't see his wealth as something that is that amazing. There are richer people than him after all. But what I do really appreciate is his ability to apply focus and attention to the things that his mind conjures and then he is able to make it happen.

There is a known cycle that happens within each of us and that cycle is either a death spiral or a leap to the top. That cycle is about the ability to have potential but lacking the belief that you can make something happen without losing too much.

Many people tend to have ideas but never actually make it because they think, "What's the use? It probably won't work." Or "What's the use? Someone else would have already thought of that." Or worse "What's the use? It's not going to be worth very much." And these kinds of thoughts feed into our psyche and we end up either not doing that which would put us on the path to greatness or it would put us on the path to saying, "See, I told you so" when it won't come to fruition. Normally, when you do not go all out, that's exactly what happens. You end up proving your doubts right. I see Musk as someone who never, even for a moment, thought that it was not possible. But what's more important – he never worried about the payoff. Once you take the payoff out of the equation – you have nothing to fear because there is no downside.

All too often, we read material that disguises itself as motivational rhetoric and feeds us with notions claiming that focusing on the reward is all the energy you need. There have been some who have evidence to point to, but I assure you that any evidence that suggests reward as the primary motivation is evidence that is ill-contrived. In Musk's case, he was hungry for contribution and achievement.

"I'm not trying to be anyone's savior. I'm just trying to think about the future and not be sad."
— Elon Musk

Maye Haldeman, Musk's mother, was born in Regina – the capital of Saskatchewan, Canada. Even from a young age, Maye was extremely attractive in appearance and vivacious in personality. Her energy was undoubtedly compounded by a family who didn't know the meaning of kicking it back or taking it easy. They couldn't necessarily be labeled as overachievers – a suspiciously pejorative term, but they were a high-impact and high-energy lot. They were always on the move and always doing things that were not typical of the average Canadian family.

Maye's parents, Winnifred and Joshua, were trailblazers even if it was just the start of the fifties in North America. History looks at the fifties in southern Canada with the same lens it looked at James Dean's America – wild, successful, and rebellious. That typically characterized the Haldeman family. They were financially well-positioned – enough to pack up and move their entire family across the world to almost wherever they wished. And, because the Haldemans were pretty adventurous and they could afford to buy their own aircraft, they packed up the family, loaded them up into that plane and flew halfway around the world to South Africa.

As the bird flies, in a straight line, that is about 8,000 miles. But if you think about it, that aircraft would not have been able to fly straight across; it needed to puddle jump and head east before coming up on Europe then flying south toward Pretoria, and that made it more like 10,000 miles. So think about that for a minute. It's not like getting on I40 and driving for three days from Nashville to Flagstaff. If you think of driving from Tennessee to the Grand Canyon in the summer, it is a brilliant experience with the kids. Try making this flight with four kids, two of whom were just two years old (Maye and her twin sister were two years old when the family made this journey.)

Maye's twin sister is someone you would have probably heard off: Kaye Rive. Yes, that's her married name. Before that, she was Kaye Haldeman. (Interesting set of names for the twins –

Maye and Kaye.) Maye went on to marry Errol Musk and became Maye Musk while Kaye became Kaye Rive, mother of Peter and Lyndon Rive of Solar City. Yes, Peter and Lyndon are Elon's cousins. Small world, ain't it?

Well, back to the cross-continent excursion that the Haldeman's took when Maye and Kaye were just two years old. It must have been one interesting flight to cross the Atlantic and the only way that a single-engine plane could do it without running out of fuel over the Atlantic would have been to hug the New England coast up the Nova Scotia then cross over to Iceland before heading over to Norway and down through mainland Europe, and from that point on it would be all overland flying except for the crossing of the Mediterranean, unless they crossed it near the Nile in Egypt and continued down all the way across the African continent until they got to South Africa. This route is good for two reasons. First of all, it is the best route to take when crossing the Atlantic in a single-engine aircraft.

You can't just plug the lats and longs into the GPS and make a straight line from Regina, Canada to Pretoria, South Africa. Well, first of all, there were no GPS satellites to transmit data, no GPS receivers to receive the sat data, and no database of maps to make sense of it all. It was, after all, the fifties. But even if you put all that aside, remember they were flying a single-engine (piston engine, nonetheless) and in the event of engine failure you need to be able to glide forward or backward, or left or right, toward land for a safe emergency landing. So, for this to happen, you always have to have land within a glide path based on your altitude. The only way to do that would be to fly at a certain altitude and hug the coast in a way that, in the event of a problem, you'd just have to glide to the coast. As safe as that is, it makes for a very long trip because you need to stop every three to four hours and fill up on Avgas. What made the trip even more interesting was that it was done by dead reckoning all the way. That means no electronic or radio navigation equipment, just good old maps, rulers, compasses, and protractors.

Grandpa Haldeman bought his aircraft and obtained his Private Pilot's license while working as a licensed chiropractor in Canada. By the way, Musk is a Private Pilot as well. Just after the sale of Zip2, around the time he bought the McLaren, he also bought a single-engine aircraft.

Back to the Haldemans.

Dr. Haldeman was a popular and well-respected member of society and had a thriving practice when he decided that Canada was not politically in lockstep with his ideals. So, he packed-up, picked-up and moved to Pretoria. Curious choice of cities but the Haldemans were looking for answers to life and nature. They were also looking for a break from the monotony of the West and the romance of the African bush. The Haldemans were of Canadian citizenry even though Joshua was from Minnesota. Maye and the other Haldeman children were born in Canada. You will see later that Elon Musk found his way to North America forty years later thanks to this fact.

Once the Haldemans got to Pretoria and got situated, it didn't stop there for the flying Haldemans. You see, Grandpa and Grandma Haldeman were looking for the lost city in the desert and they made a dozen flights crisscrossing the continent of Africa with that objective in their small single-engine plane.

But that wasn't the extent or limit of their flying. The Haldemans also flew longer journeys and navigated their way – family and all – across the globe and down toward Australia. That was approximately a 14,000-mile trip to basically travel back up to North Africa, then across Asia Minor, over India, and then down through South East Asia, down the Malay Peninsula across to Indonesia, and along the islands of New Guinea and down to Australia – all this with kids in the backseat. "Are we there yet?" takes on a whole different flavor under those circumstances.

The Haldemans were a tremendous influence on the Rive and Musk kids as they grew up close to each other and heard stories of their grandparents who took South Africa by storm. They were brave souls that were up for a good challenge.

Maye and Kaye raised their children close to each other and with a good relationship between the cousins who, as you can tell by this point, are all strong entrepreneurs in their own right. Between Elon's tech endeavors, Kimball's green adventures, and the Rive brothers' energy and so on, what you have is a family that has taken this world by storm. That is one launchpad that you should keep at the back of your mind as you size up Musk and, more importantly, try to understand him so that you can find the light in your life and make a difference, finding your unique way just as he and his siblings and cousins are doing.

Vanity Fair calls them the 'First Family of Tech.' I have to agree.

There was a lot of intellectual wattage in the Haldeman strain. Both Maye's and Kaye's kids – the Rives and the Musks – were an amazing bunch of kids who were close-knit beyond just the binds that tied them from their mothers. They had another similarity going for them beyond genetics, which was the fervor of intellectualism. Imagine having discussions with your siblings and cousins about the efficacy of banking at the age of twelve? Not exactly what I was talking about at that age. How 'bout you?

But that just goes to show the caliber of their grain. In another famous story of his youth, the cousins got together when Musk was still a teenager and they decided that they wanted to get a business up and running.

Musk was an advanced coder by the time he was twelve years old and was able to code a game that found enough interest that it was published, *and* he was paid for it. There is no doubt that he is industrious and he wants to earn a buck. But earning a quick buck is not all that interests him.

He and his bunch of siblings and cousins got together and decided they wanted to open an arcade near a school. He understood marketing very well and he understood it from a functional perspective rather than an academic one. This group of industrious kids did everything that they needed to do. They got the documents and got the lease, then put in for licensing and did everything that went along with that. A significant amount of thought and work went into it and they were on the home stretch when they came upon municipal documentation, which needed an adult over 18 to sign it. None of them had seen this coming and were totally taken aback. They didn't know where to turn to. They tried Maye, but Maye was too busy working two jobs to be able to take the time to come downtown to sign the documents. They tried Dr. Rive, but he was not only not willing, he was absolutely upset that all this had gone on without a shred of permission from any of the parents. In the end, it couldn't get off the ground because there was no adult to sign-off.

This says a lot about this group of kids. There is a lot of energy and imagination. They didn't just start down this enterprising path when they were teenagers either. This goes pretty far back to even before they were having conversations of banking and commerce amongst themselves. They put rubber to the pavement when they realized that there were so many opportunities in different layers across different dimensions – and that is how they saw it.

In one incident, they realized that chocolate was a cheap commodity in comparison to most of the other candy. It was easily affordable and this was the good chocolate, not the candy that is made to look like chocolate that you see on shelves now. The chocolate that they could get was fairly easy to find but fairly good quality. They also realized that there was a huge disparity between the cost of input – the chocolate – and the price people were willing to pay if it was in a different form. That was the first dimension.

They decided to change the form of the easily available chocolate and make it into Easter eggs and, that way, what was once just pennies could now be sold for much more. But they didn't stop there. By the time they were done, what could have sold as Easter eggs for a Rand (the unit of South African currency) they sold for ten Rand. Remember, the chocolate was just a tiny cost, melting it and shaping them into eggs demanded skill, but they could now turn around and sell it for 1 Rand – a huge profit. But they didn't just do that. Instead, it was Elon who decided to sell it for 10 Rand and, instead of just going anywhere and selling it, they went to the poshest neighborhood in Pretoria and knocked on doors, sporting their cutest smiles and smartest outfits and demanding 10 Rand for something that you could get at the store for 1 Rand. Most of the times, the differentiated clientele paid the asking price, but if in the rare event, they were asked why it was so expensive, the kids returned with a well-rehearsed line that they were enterprising and that they should be rewarded for such. They made a killing from that endeavor.

Does that sound at all familiar to you?

It should, as it's exactly what Elon did when he started selling Teslas. He peeled back the layers of commerce and understood that the wealthy will always be willing to pay more in appreciation for some things. You could then take that increased margin and reinvest it into other cars. And that's how he positioned the Tesla brand, and that's how he financed the development of production runs – by going to the rich consumer first. I have no doubt he will do that with SpaceX and their first shots to space. More on that later in the book.

The significant intellectual ability among the kids was in no small measure due to the way the Haldeman twins raised them. Both sisters have three kids. The Musks included Tosca, Kimball, and Elon, and the Rives included Lyndon, Peter, and Russel.

The one way to describe the kids was the same way you would describe their mothers and the same way you would describe the Haldemans – energy. They had pure energy coursing their veins in such abundance that they could take on almost any project and then make it happen.

I remember during the Presidential debates in 2016 – don't worry I am not going to talk politics here – Candidate Trump talked about low energy candidates, and he was right. Low energy people move slower than sloths. But the Musk and Rive family were all highly energized and, thus, had all the motivation in the world and the energy to make something happen.

There is a genetic aspect to this because, if you look at all the boys in those two families, you see the same energy that Grandpa Haldeman had in the way he made his practice a success and the way he was a popular figure in politics in his neck of the woods. You can also see that he was gung-ho in finding the lost city of the Kalahari Desert. Grandpa Haldeman passed in 1975 in an air crash chasing after the elusive lost city – Elon was still a toddler when it happened, but that same exploration-adventure gene Joshua Haldeman had was certainly passed down to his grandkids.

Maye Haldeman was an attractive young woman, just as Kaye was. She started modeling early in her career but she wasn't just one who stepped toward a life of glamor as a model like many do, as she also had a good head on her shoulders. She was as sharp intellectually as she was charming personally and Errol Musk couldn't take his eyes off her from the first time they met. She said no many times and obviously, as history tells us, his tenacity won the day. Errol was a handsome young man at the time as well and, what's more, he was equally as smart as the stunning Maye. Errol went on to become an engineer and Maye completed two Master's degrees.

Once they were married and the kids were born, Errol's business was doing well and they lived in one of Pretoria's finest neighborhoods. Errol was a civil engineer who specialized in building homes and was a strict father. If you gazed at him and just blurred your focus a little, you would look in Errol's direction and think you were looking at Elon. Elon and Errol look more like each other than Kimball and Elon do or even Kimbal and Errol.

But the similarities in looks and the ability to turn on the focus of their minds is where the similarities between the older and the younger Musk start and end. Everything else is night and day.

There is a big family secret about the way that Errol treated the kids and no one really wants to talk about it. They keep a really tight lip and that alone speaks volumes, I feel. I will get to that a little later. But, for now, what you should place at the back of your mind is that Errol, for all the stories that you may have heard, is not a bad person or a bad father. He was not even a bad husband.

If you want to take this a step further, just think about it in these terms.

Once they moved to the larger house in Pretoria and when things were going really well for the Musk family, the cracks between husband and wife started to show. The couple who were very much in love with each other, and electrically attracted to each other, had hit a few bumps and grown apart. Nine years into the marriage, the Musks separated and the children followed Maye.

But that didn't last for long because, about a year or two later, Elon asked to go live with Errol. When Maye enquired as to the reason, Elon's only reason was that a boy's place was next to his father. Soon after that, Kimball followed and, soon after that,

Tosca did as well. All three kids went back to their father and stayed there for some time.

Money was not a problem in the Musk home, and the fact that they were European in an Apartheid rule meant that they had a fairly good life. Errol took the kids on long journeys within South Africa and even abroad. They flew to countries that showed Elon and his siblings that a world outside South Africa existed and that it was abundant and amazing. One of the motivations that Errol had for doing this was the conversation Errol had with a three-year-old Elon years earlier where Elon asked his dad "Where is the whole world?" For some reason, that question and the tenacity in which Elon undertook all things made Errol want to show his son more of the world than what one could see around Pretoria.

The fact that the kids went back to their father says a lot about the dynamic that existed between them and this has been misunderstood. There is a lot of online stuff that places Errol in a bad light and that is not entirely true. How bad could he have been if the kids chose to stay with him? Think about that for a minute and you will realize that the reasons that they wanted to stay with him and the difficulties they had growing up are not even close to what is said on the internet and what is insinuated. Errol himself is a charming man with a deep intellect and an interesting sense of humor. He is full of energy and he obviously needed it because, without that, he would not have been able to keep up with Maye, who was energetic, as mentioned earlier.

Chapter 3 Paternal History

"The idea of lying on a beach as my main thing just sounds like the worst. It sounds horrible to me. I would go bonkers. I would have to be on serious drugs. I'd be super-duper bored. I like high intensity."

— Elon Musk

Errol Musk and May Haldeman divorced when Elon was nine years old. As young as he was, he was fully aware of the event, although he may not have been fully aware of the conditions precedent or the full consequences of it. From his perspective, the happy family that he saw with his pre-pubescent eyes had come to an end and he was now leaving the home he was familiar with and moving away with his mom and siblings. He still stayed in contact with his cousins and, of course, Kimball was next to him even if Maye wasn't. She was busy enough – handling two jobs to raise three children.

This part of his life had an impact as days rolled into weeks and weeks became months. As much as he loved his mother and his brother and sister, he had this deep longing in him for his father. It was unbearable and the tears that he had at that time, even though mostly in private, were tears that even he didn't fully understand.

There are two areas to note when it comes to Musk's sudden separation from his father. Although they were not that far away from each other, the fact that his presence was not under the same roof made a huge difference to a young boy who had it hard in the outside world and relied a lot on family. The second area to note was that boys – all boys – have much to learn from their fathers. It is a genetic fact, and the ones that usually feel that are the ones who are immensely in touch with their feelings or those who have hypersensitive personalities.

Elon Musk certainly lives up to his reputation of being hypersensitive. That hypersensitivity was the core reason that he retreated from social engagements and it is the same reason he was able to attach himself to the pursuit of knowledge that was presented to him. When you are hypersensitive and empathic, your only source of solace comes from the source of enjoyment that is predictable – in Musk's case, that was reading. Reading gave him a sense of certainty of calm. What he read could not hurt him or harm him but, most importantly, what he read would not overwhelm him in the same way people and events around him could.

Indeed, the world around him did overwhelm him constantly and deeply. When you have a hypersensitive personality, you tend to take in more than others do. Think about it this way; imagine your mind and senses as a water tank. And this water tank is connected to a larger water tank that contains the water. For now, just assume the smaller tank is the psyche of a person and the larger tank with the water is the world around this person.

Now, the way the two tanks are connected is via a conduit. A normal tank will have a conduit that is maybe an inch in diameter and, with this one-inch conduit, the water from the outer tank flows at a moderate pace to fill up the inner tank. So, you get that analogy, right? The stimuli from the outside world enter your psyche at a moderate pace – sight, sound, smell, and all the events that are going on around you. At this moderate pace, you can manage the incoming information stream.

For a hypersensitive or empathic person, it is like taking that same water tank set up and, instead of having one external tank draining to the internal tank via a one-inch conduit, it's like placing a dozen larger tanks and attaching it to the inner tank and connecting each of them with a conduit fifty inches in diameter.

When placed in identical surroundings, the average person and the empathic person experience very different events. The empathic person absorbs more of the surroundings while the average person doesn't. So, the average person is able to process what he perceives in a way that is manageable while the empathic person (who is not used to his power) gets overwhelmed. Empathic people who are not used to this usually retreat into themselves or do something that cuts out the rest of the streams of information. They learn to focus just so that they don't get overwhelmed. Musk was this kind of kid.

Chapter 4 The Early Years

"I came to the conclusion that we should aspire to increase the scope and scale of human consciousness in order to better understand what questions to ask. Really, the only thing that makes sense is to strive for greater collective enlightenment."

— Elon Musk

By the time he was three, Musk's parents started to notice consistently and frequently that he would withdraw into himself. They were quite concerned. Being a kid from that same generation, I can tell you that psychiatry was not what it is today. We didn't think we know what it was and so he was not diagnosed with ominous sounding ailments. They just let him be.

It turns out that Musk was empathic and he would not withdraw. Instead, he would counter the stream of input by focusing his energy on one thought or one event and he would give it his entire effort in contemplating or understanding.

The human mind is an interesting piece of work – for some of us more than others. Musk's mind is one of few living specimens that reaches a level of ability that is fairly rare and surrounded by unique circumstances. Einstein's genius came from his ability to imagine; Newton's genius came from his ability to observe things and finding ways to explain them; Edison's genius came from meticulous tracking of errors and hypothesis – a sort of meticulous process of elimination. Jobs' genius came from recognizing order and aesthetics. All the great men and women of the world have a specific brand of genius that they capitalize on. In Musk's case, his genius was rooted in his ability to direct his attention, aim his focus, and not come out of it until he gets to the point where he has fully assimilated the knowledge that he was focused on, or finds the solution he is in search of.

If you have read anything about Musk online, you will probably be in possession of the same impression that he is a genius with a photographic memory. That's true. If you know that, then you would also know that he is an avid reader. Well, calling him an avid reader would be like calling the Pope holy. His reading has been the hallmark of all that it means to be Musk. But we need to look at that ability at a microscopic level to understand these powers of reading, memory, and assimilating data to make sense of it.

When he was a kid, his father used to notice that, more often than not, Musk would stare off into space. But the thing to note was that his eyes weren't vacant and glazed over, they were intense and alive. Nevertheless, he would have no connection to the rest of the world when he was in the midst of one of these episodes. And this happened pretty often. This was before the time he could read and it was not clearly understood why, but it was taken to be a related phenomenon that was unique to just Elon among his siblings.

There are three areas that you should understand about Musk. The first is his ability to apply intense focus on whatever he was paying attention to. The second is his ability to not get distracted from that event, Finally, his ability to memorize every aspect of the event. This was certainly applicable to reading and diagrams, but not limited to them. It applied to everything his senses witnessed as long as he was paying attention.

A person's memory is fairly intuitive to understand if you pull on the right strings. In the case of memory, it's all about making neurons in the brain and then associating those neurons with other existing neurons to form associative memories and then building on top of that. We won't go into the details of memory creation or memory recollection, but a brief visit to the way Musk processes his is in order.

When you see something in passing, your mind records it. In fact, recording the memory is not always the problem. If you were exposed to a sequence of flashcards, it all gets recorded in your brain, and there are three things that happen in particular. The first is a chemical reaction that stores short-term memory in chemical format. You can think of this as the staging area. Once this is done in the hippocampus, the part of the brain that stitches events in your mind and directs the recording of the memory has to decide whether or not this memory is something that you will recollect frequently or otherwise. If it determines that you need to access this memory frequently, it will store the memory in a way that is easily accessible – in your conscious memory. If it determines that you do not need to access it often, it gets stored in a sort of subconscious memory. I say 'sort of' because the kind of memory we are talking about here feels like it is subconscious because it is not consciously accessible and you need to go to great lengths to retrieve it. There are at least two ways to determine if your brain stores it in conscious memory or in subconscious memory. The first is the manner in which it was recorded. If a lot of attention or sensitivity was applied to it, then that memory is what we say "makes an impression" and it is stored in conscious memory. If it is just absorbed in passing, then there is no intensity to it, and it then gets stored in subconscious memory and, when you need to access it, you need to get someone to hypnotize you to access that memory or you need to put a lot of effort into it. When most people find that an event is not readily accessible or still unavailable to them after a little effort, they typically give up and say they have forgotten the event. But, actually, it is still there and just takes longer and more effort to access.

In Musk's case, he remembers everything because he is super-present wherever he is and whatever he does. His intensity is unparalleled so his mind records everything and records it in the conscious memory. So much so that he seems to have a photographic memory.

Out of the three things that categorize his cerebral abilities, the part that is most important is indistinguishable from the part that we would normally categorize as less relevant. You see, all three parts of him, the undeviating attention and the intense focus, coupled with the third ability to not be distracted – meaning it's almost like you can't wake him up from a dream because none of his other sensors are connected.

Think of it this way; if I were asleep and you tried to wake me up by calling my name, when I respond to that call and wake up to fully awakened consciousness, it's only because there was a part of me that was listening to the outside world while I slept. If there was no listening going on then, no matter how loud the alert, it will not reach my mind and that will mean I can't respond and, thus, I can't wake up until something internally releases me from that slumber and I wake up on my own.

In the same way, a typical person's ability to lose themselves in a focused effort on a task is usually about 4–6 minutes and then they are internally shaken out of their state so that they can view the world around them. This was the way we evolved so that we are constantly alert about our surroundings. It is a feature that keeps us safe. We are designed to jump to alert in the event that a new stream of data comes along. But in today's world that new stream of data that takes us away from whatever we are doing is called a distraction. And the best way to focus is not to apply more energy to it, but to rather just disregard distractions. Some of us have the ability to inherently not regard distractions and others have to build it by force and discipline. In Musk's case, it came naturally.

As he started focusing on the things around him, distractions never phased him because he could not really perceive them, so he would stare and focus on something till it was done. It was the same when he saw something new, or it was the same when he was reading a book – fiction or non-fiction. When he read fiction, as he would so often do, he could not put the book down like how the average person reads. He needed to get to the end of the story and, between his curiosity and his ability to not be distracted, there was just no way of pulling him off a book until the intervening event was so great or he finished the task. And, because his focus was absolute, he stored everything he consumed in conscious memory, and that gives him the ability to recall all that he has laid eyes on. That is really the secret to his genius. The secret to his success, however, is another matter.

It doesn't end there.

Elon Musk has superior powers of analysis and understanding the subject matter for what it is. When he was in Queen's College, as well as the times when he was at Penn's Wharton School, his ability to just memorize the facts were not in doubt, but his ability to understand the fundamental nature of the knowledge that was being focused on was never really understood by his peers or teachers until they started to see his creativity and understanding come into focus.

When you have the ability to memorize, what does that get you? Well, nothing much really. You just mimic others' conclusions and you parrot others' words. But when you take superior memory and add it to the ability to understand and contextualize, then what you get is a step in the direction of genius. When you then take that and add it to the ability to imagine – which can, of course, be related back to memory, then what you have is the makings of a genius that is unlike any of the other towering successes that we have come to know. Musk is such a person. He has powerful memory, recall, understanding, and imagination.

During his college days, whether it was physics or economics, the intellect that his classmates say he exhibited was not one of just memorized and regurgitated facts and data – anyone could do that. His intelligence came in at two levels. The first level was his ability to understand the concepts he was focusing on in human terms. That means, if we look at a simple economic study of supply and demand, for example, he understood that concept beyond just the charts of sloping supply and intersecting demand curves. He instinctually absorbed the information enough to understand what it meant in practicable, actionable, and accurate human terms. The knowledge was real to him and, because of that, he was able to apply what he learned to what was already percolating in his head.

When he was at Penn, he was enrolled in two separate programs. On the one hand, he was doing physics in the School of Arts and Sciences and, on the other hand, he was doing business at the Wharton School of Business – both faculties of the University of Pennsylvania. By the way, these are both tough programs to get into, being as Penn is an Ivy League university and Wharton is the top undergraduate business program in the country.

So, he was sharpening his skills on both sides of the equation. On the one side he was looking at technology and on the other side he was looking at commercializing that technology. One of the papers he wrote for one of his classes was actually a Business Plan that talked about creating a business that would harvest solar energy from the sun. I know everyone has grand illusions of the idea but here is where Musk distinguishes himself from everyone else.

On the one hand, he was looking at it from the Utopian physics side, where there is a cleaner and more efficient world based on clean energy. That's great, most people dream of that but, in Musk's case, the physics behind his plan was spot on.

Then, on the other side of it, was the business plan that talked about the way to make it commercially viable. And that too was spot on, according to the professors that graded his paper. They looked at it and asked him to defend the science, which he did, and they looked at the business principles which were all sound. He obviously got an A for the paper, but the thing to note is that it wasn't a pie-in-the-sky kind of endeavor. It showed a depth of thought and he knew one thing for certain – he knew that to make it work, no matter how much it benefited society, the practical matter of the whole thing was that it had to make money. And it did. That's how he is with all his businesses. Look at Tesla and look at PayPal. All the businesses that he started, no matter how complex, were technically sound and financially viable. That was his winning stroke and it remains so today.

Musk's early years were not defined by the events of his childhood as much as they were corralled by the intense dataset and understanding that he had accumulated in his head. His intellect gave him the cloak he needed to shield himself from the bullying in school and the imagination gave him the wand to wish away his troubles at home. It was the perfect storm of greatness, but I am sure that, during the time he was enduring it, it seemed excruciating rather than uplifting.

His life was not a bed of roses, as you have seen to this point. From the split of the family home to the treatment he received in school from the bullies to his inability to understand the social environment around him, he could not get a grip on the only reality he knew. The beating he received in school that put him in the hospital for two weeks and made his face unrecognizable to his father was the result of the incessant bullying that he stood up to – or ran away from – depending on the odds and the situation surrounding the encounter. It got so bad that the bullies got together and gave him a good thrashing, kicking him down the stairs. This bullying thing was a systemic problem in South Africa, and his father's report to the police didn't result in much except the police saying basically, that 'boys will be boys.' No action was taken and no charges were filed, even though his father repeatedly pushed the cops to do something about it. Even the school, Bryanston High School in Pretoria, looked the other way. Years later, under the current Principle, however, they were sorry to hear how much misery their indifference had been the cause of.

That episode of the beating has been told and retold countless times across the web. The narrative of the event has taken on various shades of intensity and almost diluted its real effect and influence on Musk's life. But it was not the only event and it was not the last one. He recently revealed that he had to have surgery to correct a nasal anomaly that resulted from that particular episode. He had, until the surgery, trouble breathing because of the hindrance the injury had caused all this time later.

That single event, while having an effect on his youth, was not the driving force of his decisions, but it was the visual representation of the taunts and conditions he felt all through his school years – and that was indeed the fuel that drove him to better develop the strengths that were inherently within him. You see, bullying has a specific psychological effect on the victim. It creates a simultaneous feeling of incapability and fear. In Musk's case, it caused him to worry about his safety on a daily basis, and it told him that he was powerless. Two very negative aspects of life to have baked into a boy while he is growing up.

The national culture in South Africa is very different from the culture of the West – Canada and the United States, or pretty much the whole of Europe. What the Apartheid nationalists call European is in physical appearance only – skin color, hair, and eye features. But it has nothing to do with European values or cultures. The Apartheid South Africa that existed back in the day viewed success very differently from the way the rest of the world viewed success, and Musk instinctively understood that from a very early age. How he picked this up is not clear, but it must have been from an amalgamation of his reading and his travels, and in no small part due to his instincts telling him that there had to be a better way.

I make it a point to distinguish Apartheid South Africa from today's South Africa because the culture has completely evolved. The Apartheid South African culture that prevailed during Musk's childhood and early teenage years was a foreboding force in the lives of all that country's people and the negative effects were undiscriminating, even though government policy was.

One of these side effects was the way that success was viewed. We take it for granted that success in the United States and much of the Western world is seen as a uniform benchmark. But success is pretty much an individual's definition even if it does have national influences and cultural bias based on social norms and national conversations. Success in the United States means a lot of different things and it is very different from what it means in Tibet. For instance, success in Indonesia means something totally different than it does in Australia. Although Hollywood's pervasive influence has all but leveled the playing field today, thirty years ago definitions and corresponding actions differed.

In South Africa, entrepreneurial success was not revered; it was questioned. When someone in South Africa makes it big and makes lots of money, back then they would ask "Why do you have so much money?" In the US, the question is 'How did you do it?"

It may not seem like much, but it was part of the culture that did not appreciate or promote entrepreneurial endeavors. If the country does not promote entrepreneurship, then it is not going to be geared to providing the psychological infrastructure needed to develop and motivate budding entrepreneurs. When that is missing, those who have entrepreneurism in their blood instinctively look elsewhere for this element. That was in part what drove Musk out of Africa, as much as all the other stuff that was happening in his life.

Moving to America is not something that you should take lightly because not everyone agrees with its politics or cultural values. Errol Musk certainly didn't. When the time came for Elon to spread his wings, his father was not interested in spreading them to America. In fact, Errol reneged on a deal he made with his son to accompany him to America. It even got to the point that Errol threatened him by cutting off his funds if he were to choose to go to America. Instead, he was told that all of his educational needs and expenses would be met if he attended a local university in South Africa.

Most people that age have one of two things going for them. They either have their parents pay for college or they live in a country where financial aid for college is easily obtained. But for someone like Musk, none of that was available to him. Whatever he set out to do, he needed to do it on his own and without any aid from friends or family. Well, friends were almost non-existent and, as for family, the only one in his family that could afford to help him didn't want him going to America and so withheld the funds; and those who wanted to help him, like his mother and siblings, didn't have the funds to do so. So, he ended up relying on himself.

He could have given up and taken the easy road, but he didn't. And so, by making that choice to face the world alone at that young an age, the positive lessons of hard-knocks were backed into the fiber of his being. He matured with the skillset of someone who had adapted to fend for himself and that strengthened him, emboldening his attitude, and giving him his cloak of invincibility.

Chapter 5 Coming to North America

"I think it's important to reason from first principles rather than by analogy. The normal way we conduct our lives is we reason by analogy. [With analogy] we are doing this because it's like something else that was done, or it is like what other people are doing. [With first principles] you boil things down to the most fundamental truths... and then reason up from there."

— Elon Musk

I wish I could tell you that Musk's decision to come to America and the subsequent events were easy and that he traveled a path that was comfortable, but I can't. What Musk went through in the years following his decision and ability to get out of South Africa were some of the more difficult events I have heard of. It almost reminds me of the 1992 Cruise/Kidman movie, *Far and Away*, about a couple from Ireland who come to America during the time of the Oklahoma land rush. As hard as they had it, when you look at Musk's journey to the US by way of Canada, it almost feels harder and, if you want to appreciate what it takes to make big dreams come together, then this is something that you have to look at more than just the events and the anecdotes that you read online or in books. I mention the movie because, in Musk's case, reality was harder than fiction.

As difficult as his relationship with his father was, Musk always loved him, looked up to him and, most of all, respected him. The South African culture of bravado and macho behavior is not something that is academic, but something that is real in daily life – between friends, between family, and certainly between father and son. It was obviously worse among rivals – which is one of the reasons he was taunted and bullied. But as for the father-son relationship, it was a national bedrock principle that to teach macho, you have to be macho. And so that defined many filial relationships. That is the redeeming feature of the whole story.

There was a filial obligation that Musk was not willing to abdicate, and that was obvious throughout his time in the paternal household. But to be clear, and this has everything to do with his jump to North America, there were four distinct stages of his relationship with his father.

The first stage was the time when he was still a pre-adolescent, and this covered the period before his mother left. The second was the time when he moved out of his father's house when his parents were divorced. The third is the time that passed when he had returned to his father's house. And the last was when he left South Africa and his father behind and headed for his new life – this last part being when he saw the final fraying of their relationship. He is at a point now in his life where he has no intention of introducing his children to his father.

That decision will undoubtedly change as he matures to a point that he understands the actions his father took and, if he is able to step away from the pain, then the natural state of his being would choose to reconcile and bury the hatchet.

You already know that there were no less than three reasons that he wanted to come to the United States. On the one hand, there was the South African military conscription that he really wished to avoid. The second was that he needed to extricate himself from a life that had been horrible to him and, with such levels of psychological and physical abuse, he associated all of Pretoria, and by extension, all of South Africa as one long bad nightmare and wanted to change the view. Finally, and this was the pull when compared to the first two pushes, was that he wanted to develop his software and technical IT ability. For the man that the world now calls the next Thomas Edison, South Africa was not cutting it.

After Waterkloof House Preparatory School, followed by Bryanston High School and then an eight-month stint at the University of Pretoria in 1988, he boarded a plane, against his father's most strenuous objections, and landed in Canada. If you think his life in South Africa was tough based on what you've read thus far about Musk, then you've just scraped the surface.

What I ask you to consider is that Musk is empathic, as mentioned earlier and, if you consider the course of his life in South Africa to be painful, think about how he must have felt facing it first hand, and being an empathic who magnifies his surroundings and the events around him by a significant factor. To say that he was leaving emotional baggage behind would be an understatement. But whatever pain he felt at the time was not something that he allowed to distract him, nor did he ever feel sorry for himself.

One of the things about Musk that jumps out at a number of people who study him, his words, and his actions, is that he is, above all, one of the most resilient people you will come across. There is an old saying that comes to mind when I see him and that is 'strong trees are the result of strong winds.' Which is to say that much of what he endured as a kid was responsible for making him resilient and it also created a path for him to escape into his own mind.

The one thing that was, without a doubt, his father's contribution to his whole equation, aside from the obvious parenting, was that he took the kids with him on travels in and out of Africa. This gave Musk the idea that things were different outside his homeland and that gave him the hope he needed. He sought his father's approval and got it when he asked if his father would take him to America and make the move so that they could emigrate from South Africa. His father had the financial ability and the knowledge to pull it off, but he changed his mind at the 11th hour.

Not only that, he forbade Elon from leaving as well and incentivized him to stay by telling him that he would pay for Elon's college if he stayed in South Africa. Errol was a smart and hardworking man who did not want their wealth to tarnish the mettle of the Musk children and, in the course of doing that, came across as a hard and stubborn man. But in essence, he was doing what he thought was best for his kids.

There were numerous fights and arguments between the stubborn Elon and an even more stubborn Errol. But, in the end, the bottom line was that Errol would cut him off if he chose to go without his father's permission. Since his father had turned him down, he elicited his mother's help.

He knew that he wouldn't make it to the United States, which had strict immigration laws, but he knew he had to get started in that general direction. He had known since he was a kid that his grandfather Joshua was American by birth, but because Grandpa Haldeman didn't pass that down to his children and Maye was born in Canada and had taken up South African citizenship, he lost the ability to seek any sort of familial immigration from the INS. But he was able to find out that his mother would still get her Canadian papers and, by extension, he would be able to do the same.

He realized that was as close as he was going to get and he had to do what was necessary, so he went to the Canadian High Commission in Pretoria. He met the necessary officers, obtained the necessary paperwork, filled it all out and did all that needed to be done. His mother just had to sign the prepared paperwork and, in a few weeks, she got her papers and her passport, which he then took and started on his paperwork. In a few more short weeks, he got his Canadian paperwork as well and, the day the passport was issued, he got on a plane with less than $300 in his hand.

And so the adventure of a lifetime began, fraught with uncertainty, hardship, hard labor, little to no food and, at times, no place to sleep. You could say that it was a time in his life when Musk had nothing but for the shirt on his back and bag on his shoulders, with no roof over his head and a future that was so uncertain that the only thing that he had to look at was the dream of how it might transpire.

But in spite all this, he felt free, and he felt that he was on his way. None of the typical comforts of the world that most 19-year-olds crave were at the top of his mind. None of the worries and need for certainties that most adults crave distracted him from his current predicament. All he had to do was stay back in Pretoria and his father would have taken care of all of it. The bullying had stopped; just a couple of years in the military and a South African degree would have meant that he would have been hired with next to no difficulty and he would have been able to continue the father's business if he so chose. It would have been a cushy and easy life. But it would have been hell for him. He liked where he was, even if it did mean sleeping at the bus station or riding in a bus on unending journeys so that he could stay warm.

Of course, he didn't plan on doing all this when he left Pretoria. He hopped on a flight to Canada with the hopes of locating an uncle that lived there. Common sense today would dictate that you get in touch with this uncle before departing Pretoria but Musk was in a hurry and all he had was a phone number. However, his mother did write her brother and told him that his nephew was making his way up there at some point after he got his passport. But they never heard back until the day

Elon boarded for Montreal. When he got there and called the number, the line was dead, so he called his mom back in Pretoria, from a pay phone. Letters had crossed while Musk was en-route and his uncle had responded that he had moved back to Minnesota and was no longer in Montreal. That now meant that Musk had nowhere to live.

What does a 19-year-old do in a strange city that he has never been to with very little cash in his pocket – and no plan? Well, Elon headed over to the nearest youth hostel and spent the night, recollecting his thoughts and regrouping. He found out that there was a bus service in Canada where you could purchase a month's pass and you could take the bus across any of its routes at any time in that period of a month. That was the cheapest housing you could get if you think about it. You hop on a bus, without any care where it was going, and what you have is a comfortable seat and warmth. You could sleep and, whenever the bus stopped, you could get food.

Not many people would think of that. What that also did was make it possible for him to scour the entire country for any relative that he could find. Every time he stopped at a town that he thought there might be family, he would get to the pay phone, pull up the directory (in those days payphones had directories; today you hardly find payphones much less directories attached to them) and start looking for all the last names that he could relate to his family. Talk about resilience and resourcefulness.

So, Musk gets on the bus and spends a few days crisscrossing the country, stopping to check payphones and cold-calling possible relatives out of the blue. Let me ask you this at this juncture, how willing are you to pick up the phone and randomly call strangers with a specific last name and ask them for a favor? I certainly couldn't, but Musk had no qualms doing it. That's why he is worth about 20 billion dollars, and counting, I guess. The will to do what is necessary.

But nonetheless, he kept trying and, after trekking about 2,000 miles from Montreal on and off buses, he got to a town called Swift Current, which was just off Highway 1. Swift Current is a small town of 15,000 residents (back in the early 90s); today the population is over 16,000 and it continues to be a wholesome, laidback Saskatchewan town. Just as he'd been doing, he got off the bus, found the telephone directory and scoured it till he found the name Teulon. It turned out that he'd hit the jackpot – it was indeed his cousin, Mark Teulon, and Teulon had a grain farm just outside of Swift Current, in a village called Waldeck, just 18 miles northwest of town.

He hitched a ride out to the farm where his cousin lived, introduced himself and asked for work if there was any. Considering he was family, even though they had never met, they found stuff for him to do. He was still seventeen (a few weeks short of 18) and eager to do just about anything.

He was happy to be off the bus and in a home where he knew that there was some measure of protection and some semblance of normalcy – a job, a bed, a roof, and homecooked meals. It was a place where he could pay his way for the basics in life without having to worry about his dwindling reserves.

He stayed in Waldeck for about a month and a half before moving on, but while he was there, he did two things. First, he worked hard moving stuff and cleaning stores and barns. The second is that he made an impression on his cousins – an impression that this kid was different from any other kid. He was indeed brighter than most and was hardworking as well – a rare and prized combination.

Chapter 6 Tending the Barn and Shoveling the Furnace

"In terms of the Internet, it's like humanity acquiring a collective nervous system. Whereas previously we were more like a [?], like a collection of cells that communicated by diffusion. With the advent of the Internet, it was suddenly like we got a nervous system. It's a hugely impactful thing."

— Elon Musk

While Musk was in Waldeck, working at the grain farm, he celebrated his 18th birthday with his new-found family. It was one of the good times that he remembers fondly and it proved the starting line in a sprint that would see him accepted to the University of Pennsylvania with a scholarship and admittance to the prestigious Wharton School of Business.

This period was also the time in which he was waiting for the rest of his family to emigrate from South Africa. His father was certainly not coming, but there was a good chance that his mother and siblings were going to follow the path that Elon had taken.

It was just a matter of time before they would make the decision and they would make the journey, but for now, Musk was on his own. He was in a new place at a new time in his life, and he was like a fish out of water with the mannerisms and the local culture. On the other hand, for those who are slow on the uptake, being thrown into a new situation may be a little difficult to handle because they are not used to the new surroundings and that makes them incapable of responding correctly. However, for a person who stores everything in the conscious part of his brain, he is quick to adapt and quick to take on the new attributes of his surroundings, melding into the fabric of his new surroundings and then excelling at doing what he was meant to do. He is the quintessential definition of being adaptive.

In archeology, there is a well-known theory that describes the survivability of a species along evolutionary lines. This is the existence of three facts in survival. It concerns when the environment changes – and by environment, I mean your physical surroundings and your circumstances. For us human beings, we have two kinds of environments that affect us significantly. The first kind of environment is the physical environment that we are subjected to. A person living in the North Pole will find it excruciating and, in some cases, deadly to migrate and live in tropical conditions.

The other environment is the cultural and cerebral environment. If we have cultural practices that are significantly different from those surrounding us, it becomes difficult to thrive because we are a species that lives on a community consensus. We live on the approval of others whether we realize it or not. Of course, there are a few of us who are contrarian in nature, but contrarians are few and far between.

The bottom line is that in order to advance our own objectives and promote our own aspirations, we need to be able to adapt to our surroundings. As much as Musk was enthusiastic about leaving Pretoria, he was also born and bred there and, as much as he didn't like their politics or appreciate their mannerisms, he was still dyed in the wool with it. The change in the new surroundings was very much real to him when he arrived, and he had to adapt to make sense of it all and make it work in his favor.

If you want to understand Musk and you, by chance, want to learn from the path that he took, then the thing that you need to come to terms with is the ability to adapt. That is one of the three things that make animals survive in the event that a change in the environment occurs. Because, when your surroundings change, you can do one of three things. You can die because you are incapable of recognizing the change and doing something about it, or you can move to a place that agrees with you, or you can adapt. The dinosaurs either perished or adapted when the environment around them changed. Polar bears will either adapt and become grizzlies as the ice of the poles recedes, or they will sink into the waters that displace the ice. What you do depends on how you see those changes and how you adapt.

Musk is a master of blending in with his surroundings – be it the physical surroundings or the cultural ones. Whether that blending in uses subterfuge and camouflage to disappear in school when hiding from bullies, or else adapting to cultural and geographic changes when he first arrived in Canada. But that ability to blend, to adapt, and to not just survive but thrive, is something we all need to take a good look at and understand how he does it because it is one of the central beams in his foundations of success.

Until Waldeck, Musk had not spent a single minute tending barns, or agricultural machinery. Until Waldeck, he hadn't known how to wield a ho, fork, a rake, or maneuver a truck. But he learned quickly, and he did so with enthusiastic fervor. It was not as though this was to be his chosen profession. It was not as though he came to Canada to learn the farming business and set up a farm, but you wouldn't be able to tell that by looking at him and how he went about his work. He was still razor sharp and smart as a whip so he blended in by learning how to do what he had to do, and he did all of it well.

Some have analyzed this part of his life as a strict work ethic, meaning that he would do whatever he has to do while he has promised to do it, regardless of how he feels about the nature of his work. You will see this as he moves on in Canada and as we unfold the story of his job history before he gets to college again. But what it could also be, and this is what some of the analysts think based on personal knowledge of his drive and habits, is that he is the kind of person who does a job well and is automatically good at it because he can be. He has the extra capacity in his head and the fact that he is empathic allows him to have a much wider field of appreciation for the facts that come his way, whereas with the normal person the facts lay dormant in front of them rather than flying at them the way they do with an empath like Musk.

The times he spent with his cousin and the family spanned just six weeks, in which time he became fairly close to them and imparted an impression on the family that this young man would one day make something of himself. But even they, in their wildest dreams, would not know how far and wide his achievements would stretch to influence this generation and the world at large. It tickles me to think what they must have been thinking or what they must have been saying to each other as they watched the launch of Falcon Heavy.

The Teulons and Musk made it a practice to sit back after dinner at the table after long days of work in the field and talk about all kinds of things, to which Musk had much to contribute. They talked about space, electricity, pollution, and a number of ideas that were close to the heart of this young man. It didn't bother anyone that this boy was a farm hand by day and intellectual prophet by night.

What seemed to lend him credibility was that the things he learned and the rate that he learned them at was beyond more than what most people could accomplish in weeks. This gave those who watched him pick up things by day the confidence that what he said in the evenings had to be credible. That's human nature as, if you can build credibility in one area, you will slowly build credibility in others. Just as his ability to develop an online payment mechanism was enough to lend him the chops needed to get credibility behind his idea for space exploration.

Musk is acutely aware of this. He understands very well that performance and reputation in one area lends itself to others. That is one of the main reasons he has staked out a very powerful niche in his life. He has crafted his public relations persona to be that of a genius, and it works. Don't get me wrong, he is indeed very smart, and he does have a photographic memory and is able to do quite a bit, but the thing that you must know is that he is no Einstein.

There is a caveat that I have mentioned in passing across the length of this book and will continue to do as you traverse its pages. As much as Musk has a lot to teach us, he is not the prophet that he makes himself out to be. He is smart, he has a photographic memory, and he works hard. But he is not the Einstein or Hawking of this world. The ideas he has developed are not earth-shattering or groundbreaking – but they are inspiring. He didn't build a new spaceship to launch into space, and he didn't take new technology to build an electric car – he took what was already available and tinkered with it. It's not like what he did with PayPal – that was an original idea but then, again, that idea was also percolating in the mind of another company that was eventually in direct competition with PayPal.

The point that I am trying to make is that, before you go ahead and jump all in trying to be Musk, you should know exactly what and who he is and what he has done to get to where he is today. When you know the truth, then you know what to emulate and what to leave out.

To those who are watching and observing, he comes across as someone who is intelligent and grounded. To those who aren't paying attention, they see a crazy man rambling incoherently from one subject to the next at the speed of thought. But here is where he makes the difference. Most people who ramble at the speed of thought live in their heads – just as Musk does. But the difference between Musk and the man that lives in his head with all the bright ideas is that Musk comes out and makes it happen. He converts inspiration and thought into tangible reality.

If he chooses to play up his intellect and genius, so be it. But for us, we will be best served to emulate his ability to absorb and his willingness to do.

If you look at his time at Teulon's farm, or if you look at his time in school where he had to hide from bullies, or if you have to look at any of the other things that have materialized in his life, you will start to realize that he has definitely and defiantly not played the hand he was dealt but rather worked to escape his status quo and create the reality his mind longed for. He is worth every red cent of the twenty billion he is valued at (based on December 2017 valuations) because nothing he has done came easily.

When a month had passed, and he was still in Waldeck, his instincts started to stir. He felt stronger and more adept with the Canadian ways, and he was still not done with his quest – which, if you recall, was to find his way into the United States. But, for now, the opportunity had yet to present itself, so he knew he had to keep moving and keep working. His family had still not joined him, and he was still all alone. He saved what he could from the wages he got at Teulon's and then began his trek westward.

If you understand Canadian Geography, you will realize that trekking from Swift Current to Vancouver is like going from Billings, Montana to Portland, Oregon. They're about the same location longitudinally speaking and work out to be a 1,500-mile westward road trip to the Pacific coast. That slow bus trip lasting days to get to his destination is a long cry from the fast private jet he flies these days that gets him to DC and back overnight.

Speaking of private jets, Musk recently took delivery of a top of the line Gulfstream 650 Extended Range. The plane typically costs 65 million dollars, in addition to the cost of maintaining a flight crew. It also emits more carbon dioxide on the ground waiting to taxi for take-off than all his Teslas do in a lifetime. Just one of the interesting contradictions in his life that I thought was rather funny.

When he got to Vancouver, the only job he could find was cutting logs. It was a good thing he had learned to use a chainsaw on his cousin's spread and so, with a little bit of training, he was able to wield the chainsaw and got cracking with a new job that paid a little more. Make no mistake about it; this was heavy work. It required a lot of intense physical labor and it required the stamina to keep pushing from one task to the next for an entire workday. Musk was not scrawny in his teenage years for long. He had soon broadened out and built up in his late teens, and his job now, carving timber into logs, presented a significant upper body workout.

When I look across the terrain that is made up of all the successful people who have made it in their life, I see that there are two factors that drive people to do what they do. They may go about doing it differently using different parts of their endowments, but the same characteristic seems to always appear when I analyze men of substantial achievement. The first one is fear. The second is ego. Musk has plenty of both. If you have them, don't let anyone tell you that they are a harbinger of failure; they are the stilts to success – if used correctly.

Mind you, this is not a matter to judge or a matter to ridicule. This is human nature. When we tell our kids to do well in school, what do we do? Many parents instinctively instill the fear of failure and the consequence of not doing well. How do the kids respond? Well, they respond by trying harder, or they get stressed. Why? Because they now fear the consequences. Fear can be a powerful motivator. Fear unlocks the hidden strength that we have to go the extra mile and squeeze the extra Joule of energy. It is not just psychological; it is visceral and, more importantly, it is chemical. If you can bring your fear online and extract the energy that derives, then you are going to be able to push harder, overcome internal hurdles and insulate against fatigue and laziness.

In The Batman trilogy's, *The Dark Knight Rises*, there is a scene where Bruce Wayne contemplates escaping from the subterranean prison. At this point, he has tried and failed and, when asked about his fear, his answer is that he fears nothing. Seems like a heroic answer, but the advice he gets in return is that to be able to push himself to squeeze out that incremental level of energy that will launch him to where he needs to be, he needs to embrace the fear. Fear unlocks the edge you need to succeed.

Think about that for a minute. Fear is the reason we have fight or flight responses. Fear is the reason we push for survival. Fear is one of the drivers that pushes Musk. But before you go around calling him a scaredy cat, I urge you to read on and get a full grasp of what we mean when we refer to Musk's fear.

Based on his words and deeds and by parsing some of the things that he says and the way he says it, you can detect that there are certain issues that have an irrational bearing on him. For instance, most of what he is extremely fearful of is what other people think of him, and he goes out of his way to make sure that he shapes that narrative. When Ashley Vance wrote the book about him, he was not inclined to green-light the book. But when he realized that Vance was going to write the book one way or the other, he decided to meet with him and place the condition that the manuscript required his approval. When Vance didn't agree to that he finally gave in but wanted to proof the manuscript. Vance didn't budge on that point either. So, a lobster and half a steak later, Musk agreed to relinquish control of the book. But today, Musk and Vance are no longer on speaking terms (after meeting frequently and religiously to discuss the book over the course of the project) because one part of Vance's narrative didn't sit well with Musk. He had ceded control of the narrative and while most of what was said was within his construct, what was outside was painful for him.

His view of himself is not just about ego for the most part. There is that too. But it is mostly borne out of fear that people won't see him as a genius. Musk needs that to thrive. That is really important to him, just as Donald Trump needs everyone to see that he is a 'stable genius' who invented the art of deal-making. It's not about over-compensation. It's about how they see themselves. They see themselves through other people's eyes. So, if other's see them as a brilliant mind, then they see themselves that way too, and seeing themselves that way helps to support their own view and raise their levels of confidence, which then allows them to go out and accomplish things.

These are all personas that we create, and we want the facts to support this creation in our mind. We tend to go to great lengths to make sure that we keep this up so that we can derive strength and, subconsciously, we fear the breakdown of that personality to the outside world and, to a large extent, the ramifications of how we see ourselves in the mirror.

His view of his own narrative feeds him to push himself and excel even more. He also has the energy to do it and the bravado to feel that he can do more than anyone else. You can see his ability to push himself no matter how tough the circumstances get. Here are two instances that come to mind right off the bat when we think of Musk along these lines. The first is the job that he took after his logging job in Vancouver.

After some time logging, he decided he needed something that paid a little more and so he went to the employment office and put in for a job.

He asked the clerk to show him the list they had and asked which one paid the most. He was in luck. He found a job that was paying almost $20 an hour and the company still had vacancies to fill.

I can tell you this though; not many people would take this job. I know I wouldn't, but Musk went down to the company and spoke to the guy in charge. He was warned that he should know what he was getting into. The company was skeptical of hiring Musk because they know that a lot of people typically apply for the job, but most of them leave in short order. It was a demanding job and had an attrition rate of about 90%.

The manager took Musk to the plant and brought him around to the furnace, then asked him again if he was certain that he wanted the job. Musk was not even the least hesitant. He wanted a higher paying job so that he could save more and get on with his life.

They hired him and 29 other people. The job was not only tough, but hazardous. It entailed him crawling through a furnace conduit and entering a small space where the furnace was ejecting hot molten gunk. His job was to shovel that ejector molten out through the passage that he came in through. Someone on the other side of the conduit would then shovel that out onto containers for disposal. No man was allowed to be in that space for more than half an hour because the heat, between the furnace, the ejector material, and the hazmat suit that they were wearing to be in there, made it uninhabitable. Most people couldn't even take it for 20 minutes. Within the first few days, only 3 out of the 30 that were hired remained at the job – Musk was one of them. Resilient!

The story itself is an interesting anecdote. It shows a person who is not afraid to get down and dirty as long as it served his purpose and contributed to the endgame. The fear that we talked about in Musk is not a fear of bodily survival but the survival of the ego that is more important.

The second anecdote that speaks to his fears, and a comparison to the misunderstanding, is the fear that he had when he had run out of cash and his companies were burning $4 million a month without an end in sight and without a solution to overcome.

This was a period in his life, during his first marriage, when everything that could go wrong was going terribly wrong. He was borrowing money wherever he could, and the fear in his eyes was easily recognizable. He had lost more weight than he had even when he was working in the furnace, and he was looking haggard with sunken eyes and pale from lack of sleep. The fear he felt here was more than he felt at any other time in his life because what was at stake was not just his life, but his narrative – and by this I don't mean to mock him or deride his priorities, I am merely showing how Musk is the kind of person who cares more for his cerebral achievement and what people think of that than he does about his personal safety – and that is why he achieves things most people can't. We are afraid of the wrong things. We are afraid of losing our life but not afraid of wasting our minds.

The time he spent roaming the lands in his new home came to an end shortly after this experience. His mother and family, minus his father, arrived in Canada and the Musks were reunited. Musk and his younger brother were always close and the two fed off each other and drove each other to succeed. Kimbal was the counterpoint to Elon's demeanor and energy. Think of Kimbal and Elon together making the perfect individual. What one lacked, the other made up for and together they could do anything. That was known to them as well. They felt an uptick in their own energies once they were next to each other. It was obvious to anyone close to both brothers. Both were smart, but the older was sharper and the younger was vibrant. Both were business minded; one was practical, the other excelled at theory.

It's easy to get the wrong idea about Musk when you read the stories and anecdotes that are out there about him. So, let's clear some of that up right now. He is definitely a resilient person, but he is not the innovator that the narrative suggests. His inspiration comes from the times reads about and the comics he grew up on. But that does not make him any less of an achiever, and that is the point that all you folks out there need to realize. You don't need to be an Edison, or an Einstein, or a Nash and come up with an original idea that no one has thought of. You can even come up with ways to do things with existing elements. Just shuffling what is on the rack gets old products to do new things.

When Musk decided he wanted to reach for the stars, he didn't decide to design his own rockets. Instead, he went to Russia and looked at the old ICBMs. He then looked at the engines that were already in existence in the US. From those, he picked out the Apollo designs and then used the core design to build the Merlin engines that powered the Falcon and the Falcon Heavy. I am not saying that he poached technology or copied. I am saying that he used off the rack items, made modifications and used software heavily to accomplish cost savings. That is a special kind of intellect in and of itself.

So, my point is that we all don't need to reinvent the wheel, but we can use the same wheel to create something better. That is Musk, in essence.

Chapter 7 Queen's University

"It is important to view knowledge as sort of a semantic tree – make sure you understand the fundamental principles, i.e. the trunk and big branches, before you get into the leaves' details or there is nothing for them to hang on to."

— Elon Musk

As the academic year rolled around, Musk made plans to head back to school. He had two options to choose from. He had to decide between the University of Waterloo and Queen's University. Both were a stone's throw from the US border and located on either side of Lake Ontario. Queen's is located in Kingston, Ontario, east of Lake Ontario, while Waterloo is located on the western shore of Lake Ontario. Musk had the good sense to visit the schools before deciding which one to attend, and he was planning on enrolling in the engineering program in Waterloo. At that point, Queen's was not his first priority. What he saw when he visited was that Waterloo was populated predominantly by guys, while Queen's had a healthy mix of good-looking women.

So, it is no surprise which one he chose and for what reason. His own words described his choice in an interview just a few years ago when he admitted that he was desperately looking forward to the opportunity to be in the mix with a target-rich environment and, if nothing else, why else attend college?

Queen's is considered to be one of the top schools in Canada, constantly achieving top-ten status in nationwide rankings. Its economics program is one of the best, and major companies typically scout for future employees here. But Musk was a technical person, in most part, until this point. In fact, if he had chosen Waterloo, his intended major would have been physics and engineering. So, what gives?

The decision was primarily made because Queen's had a better economics program than an engineering program, and the factor that tipped the scale was the fact that there were more women at Queen's then there were at Waterloo. (Note to the Admissions officers at Waterloo: you might want to rethink your admission policies and get more women.)

Musk's time at Queen's enhanced his life in a number of ways. The first was that it put him in the mix with a new culture that he had not yet experienced. Remember, all this time he had been in Canada and was close to the earth – meaning he was working with his hands and muscle, toiling away and that is a very different surrounding and very different experience from exercising your mind and imagination. Therefore, the culture during that time was much different from the culture at Queen's. For one thing, the average age at Queen's was much lower than the working world outside. The second, there was a mix of genders and he was finally able to set his eyes on the opposite sex. The third was that he could move his mind from the tangible chores to intangible inspirations. It was something that Musk had wanted to do but the reality was still not complete.

Think about this for a minute and this will help you with your aspirations as well. His idea to move stateside was not for nothing. It was not a Hollywood-driven, job-searching itch. It was because he wanted to alter his surroundings to include people that could move him deeper in an area that he had significant interest in – technology.

At heart, Musk was a technocrat, from the time he picked up science fiction comics, and still remains as such today. Much of his visions and ideas are really manifestations of the comics he poured over as a kid. He sees technology very differently from most people around the world – certainly more than his contemporaries in South Africa did at the time, and he sees it very differently from the way most people do today. But that is changing as Millennials have moved the needle in the appreciation of technology and how it is used in this day and age. Nonetheless, that's beyond the scope of this book.

Coming back to Musk and his developmental years.

There are two ways you can see college. One way is to look at it as a trove of resources conducive to the development of your own thoughts. If you look at the likes of Einstein, Nash, and other towering academic luminaries, what you find is that their time in academic institutions is not spent going to classes and slogging through homework and assignments – the true greats rarely attend class (kind of like what Bill Gates and Steve Jobs did as well) and spend their time in other pursuits, only stopping to get homework and assignments from their roommates to make sure that they do the absolute minimum to get through classes.

Musk's engagement with Queen's was no different. He rarely attended classes but still managed to ace those that he felt were important to his development. The quality that he started to display during his freshman year at Queen's was that he could understand topics beyond their academic descriptions. Take, for example, his economics classes and his introduction to supply and demand curves. He didn't just see them as mathematical graphs of lines positively and negatively sloped and met at the point of equilibrium. That's what most students to. But for Musk, he understood the human nature behind it and the reason the demand curve sloped the way it did, going lower as it moved to the left. He also understood the propensity for the supply line to rise at it moved to the left. Not only did he see it from the mathematical and theoretical positions, but he related the underlying concept to human thought and behavior patterns.

To say that he aced his economics would be an understatement – he more than understood the principles, he internalized them, allowing him to develop his own theories and his own thoughts on any given matter. You don't always find a student with the same frame of reference or the same level of understanding as Musk. Even his younger brother, as smart as he was, couldn't hold a light to the older Musk.

Universities are a great place to develop in many ways – academic and otherwise, because they put individual intellectual and inherent ability in competition with others. A campus ground serves more than just a venue for buildings, but rather they serve as an arena to pit one's thoughts against others. These competitions of cerebral matters etch out the truth, showcasing the development of humanity and technology alike.

Musk was easy to get along with in college. He still is these days, but there is a palpable difference in how he makes new acquaintances. He has come to experience the duplicity of human friendship; the same deficiency in trust that could be expected in those you call friends. His view of friendship has grown and altered in time as has his view of family. He went from trusting both friend and family alike until his friend betrayed him in outing his location to the bullies that beat him within an inch of his life. From that point on, things started to change a little. He didn't trust many people outside his own clan.

He was also severely disappointed by the actions of his father in changing his mind about moving to the United States. His frustrations as a young teenager shone a light on a determination to make himself self-sufficient and to be able to do for others what he had hoped others would do for him.

Take, for instance, the way he feels about public school. Public school, unlike university, has two major issues for Musk. The first is that public school does not create a fertile ground for the installation of knowledge or for the development of the mind. The second is that primary education mixes too many different elements that are not always good for the development of the mind. Look at how he structured the development of his own children. Instead of leaving them in regular educational institutions, even though they were private institutions that were top dollar, he was still not happy with the way it was conducted. In pursuance of that line of thinking, what he did was to pull them out of school and built a new school according to his philosophy of learning. It is very evident that he had significant thoughts of primary learning in this present frame of mind, but that frame of mind was fostered and advanced during his time in college, both during his time at Queen's and his time at Penn.

He doesn't trust the system to develop the minds of his children, and he does indeed have a point. You see, Musk is the quintessential innovator. This means that he is not one to come up with something mind-bending and far-reaching – he is no Einstein. But he will come up with something that is far enough off on the horizon that makes sense to the imagination of the masses. He takes that and finds a way to make it work. That is the construct of his mind and, since the time he has been a kid in Pretoria and with what he sees in schools today, he understands clearly that the concept of mass education robs the student of truly innovative thought.

The mind of a child is like the development of a computer program – the way Musk sees it. It requires the necessary structure, framework, and libraries to get the program to work well. The schools provide the set of libraries that the student needs to be able to handle life in the life after they graduate. And in Musk's opinion, the schools today are not doing a good enough job of providing the right algorithms or the right libraries to make that happen. As such, he decided to create his own. He has been this way even since college.

If the class that he was taking didn't provide him with the right set of 'libraries,' meaning that it didn't give him the resources to understand the subject matter in totality, then he would just extract himself, go out and find a place that would provide him with what he needed – he usually found that at the library.

There are significant trust issues that Musk has and it showed in college. As romantic as he is and as intelligent as he is, the thing that worked out in his mathematically precise mind was the fact that human beings cannot be trusted. He really doesn't trust anyone. Not his wife (first and second), not his friends and, to a certain extent, not even his own family.

He had a small group of close friends in college, but he kept away from too much socializing. He did seem to be on a mission to get a girlfriend, and he was definitely the kind of person that looked for a trophy as well as a confidant.

Let me explain.

His choice of women, and mind you, he was not even 19 at this point, were the lookers. The ones that looked really good and knew how to carry themselves. You would think that someone like Musk who was so intellectually inclined would be on the lookout for someone who would match his intellectual ability and fervor. But it turns out that Musk is not that kind of a guy when it comes to his choice in women and his choice in life partners. There are some who say that he has tried to suppress his tendencies to be gay, but that is just conjecture and unproven. But if true that doesn't imply that he is gay; it just implies that he is uncomfortable with the thought that there is a possibility that others might think that he might be gay.

To compensate, Musk has always been the kind to want to be seen with the best-looking women with the best-looking presentation. Other books have chronicled how he met his first wife, who was also a student at Queen's and I won't go too much into that except to say that he pursued her relentlessly, and she was fascinated by the romantic streak in him.

He spent two years in Kingston, most of it outside the classroom. He showed up for exams and handed in papers and still beat everyone else in the class. He had made considerable strides in his development, but the metamorphosis was not yet complete.

While at Queen's he made money on the side by building and selling computers to his dorm and classmates. If they needed to upgrade their computers he would do it for them, or if they needed to fix them, he would easily accomplish that as well. The specialty he engaged in was building game boxes for his friends and everyone around campus new that Musk was the kid to go to when they needed a computer or needed it to be fixed. He made it a point to charge prices based on the rarity of the problem. If it was an easy problem to fix, the price was low. If the problem was not common, then it got expensive. If they wanted to build a new machine to play games, then he would charge them for the build, plus he would scalp the price of the parts. He managed to save up this way with a lot of what he did and, that way, he was able to have a lifestyle that was comfortable without having to rely on anyone. He was supporting himself ever since he landed in Canada – now was no different.

Even though he was Canadian, Musk lived on the International floor at his dorm residence in Victoria Hall. It was there he met Navaid Farooq. There are two ironies here. The first is that Musk, while being Canadian, had never lived in Canada and so found the benefit of living around other International students. His to-be best friend Farooq was also on the International floor but, unlike Musk, Farooq was a natural-born Canadian, though lived overseas all his life. So, both men were Canadian but had no idea what it meant to be such. And so, that became the bond that bound the two of them.

Farooq was no lackey either. His ability to be academically advanced ahead of his classmates was well documented, but he was no match for the unbeatable Musk. The irony extended to the point that the two were paired because of their life experience. One was a Canadian all his life while the other was a new Canadian and both had no idea what that meant.

Farooq was in the Faculty of Arts and Sciences while Musk wasn't, but they did share a couple of classes together and, whenever possible, Musk would lean on Farooq for his notes and homework. But in the end, Musk would still beat him out in exams. Musk would score in the high 90s while Farooq would score in the low 90s. Even Justine and Musk would be in competition along with Farooq, and there was a time when Musk beat them all by scoring a 98 on an exam. Even though he beat them, he wasn't happy with the score, so he went and spoke to the professor and debated his point till he got a hundred.

These days, Queen's still looks back at him favorably and keeps a kind nickname for him – Rocket Man.

Musk left Kingston at the end of his Sophomore year to take up the rest of his education at the University of Pennsylvania. He was accepted with full scholarship to the Faculty of Arts and Sciences to pursue a degree in Physics. He went on to get a double degree in Economics as well from the Wharton School.

It only took two and a half years from the day he landed in Canada in hopes of meeting his uncle, and now he was making his way into the United States. From grain farms to toxic furnaces, to girls and books, he was finally making it across the northern border and into the United States. His journey had just begun.

Chapter 8 Justine

"I could go and buy one of the islands in the Bahamas and turn it into my personal fiefdom, but I am much more interested in trying to build and create a new company."

— Elon Musk

This part of the book starts with a look into Musk's personal life as it relates to the loves and love interests of his life. It is not intended to spread gossip – salacious or otherwise – but it is intended to describe the part of the man that is more personal. How you find a man in his natural state in these shadows is a good measure of the true nature of the man. How he pursues, treats, and leaves the women in his life reveals a lot about how he thinks of himself and the people around him.

It's fairly easy in today's world to sculpt your own PR and to lay the trail for the public to form an opinion of you that conforms to the way you see yourself. If you are computer savvy and have a vision, it is easy enough to do. Both these things we know Musk has in abundance. So, to really get an understanding of him you need to do three things. You need to pour over volumes of data going back to the time when he was a kid. Then you have to take that information and filter it through your own senses – sort of a way to pass any smell test. Then, finally, you have to balance what those close to him say with what those who are apart from him say – but, even more importantly, we need to find a pattern of what is uttered versus what is performed.

It's like deciphering a coded message. If you find that the message reads C but actually means A, and a little while later it reads K and actually means I, then you know that you need to spring back two letters to get the real story. In the same way, when a person says A but does E, and says E but does J, then you can get an idea of what to do and how to tweak the words into a credible prognostication of the action to come.

How Musk sees himself is a function of how he wants others to see him, and that in turn is a function of the vision he has in his head. That vision is highly detailed and specific all the way down to the color of the hair his wife – whomever she may be at the time – should have.

Justine was Musk's first wife whom he met at Queen's and pursued to the ends of the earth. He was the exact opposite of what she was looking for in a guy, and she was exactly (short of being a blonde) what he pictured in a woman – strong, smart, and attractive. They say that men eventually marry women that resemble their mothers. Freudian psychobabble aside, you can see why Justine fits this aphorism. Maye Haldeman is smart – a woman with two Master's degrees and a self-made nutritionist. She is also a model. I can't say 'was' a model, because, even in her late sixties she just recently appeared as a cover girl for a famous top-shelf magazine. So, in saying that he saw in Justine all the things that his mother was – strong, smart and attractive – wouldn't be too much of a stretch. What's even more perplexing is that he divorced Justine as well. Just like how his parents had.

Much of Musk's persona when it comes to women seems to be stuck in a loop that begins with his mother. Maye had brownish-blondish hair as a kid that darkened in her life then became more blonde over time. The older she got, the more blonde to platinum it became, and it really suits her. It is a color that imparts a distinguished and elegant look. Musk definitely defines those qualities with the measure of his mom's hair as he insists on the women that he is with to ever increasingly dye their hair blonde to platinum. He tends to show these glimpses of living in a loop by these actions.

There were many parallels between Musk and his father in how they sought and found their life partners. The immense effort that Errol put into his pursuit of Maye was bested by the effort that Musk put in with Justine. In her own words, Justine was totally set up to go after the bad boy. She liked significantly older men for their intellect and stability, and she had just been in a long-term relationship with a much older man – a sort of James Dean meets William Shakespeare kind of guy. Musk is none of that, but he was persistent. The one thing that Justine brings to the table in an effort to understand Musk better than anyone else is that she had a front and center view in that point of his life where he blossomed from the repressive days of Pretoria to the exercising and blossoming of his mental acuity. She saw him rise to towering heights academically, and she saw him fall flat during the troubled days of Tesla and Space X.

She caught his eye across a room once. Justine is tall and has long wavy hair – or at least that's how she was back then. She was certainly the most attractive soul in all of Kingston – undoubtedly so to Musk. She was also a Freshman when Musk was a Sophomore. The year difference in class was totally made up by the fact that she was far ahead of her peers when it came to literary talents. She was well aware that the kids at college were attracted to her slim waist and long sultry hair. There were more than just a few potential suitors who made their advances, but she easily brushed them off without a moment's hesitation.

He didn't have much experience with this kind of thing, and the only thing that he knew to do was to walk straight up to her. But he didn't do that before getting some background on her. The one thing Musk was good at was gathering intelligence. He got most of the story and how most of the guys failed to before getting even a word in; he decided that his attack strategy would be to play on the possibility that they had met before. Sly, but effective – or so it seemed.

He had looked around and, while he flew reconnaissance, he found out which were the parties that she liked going to. So, he waited for his chance and what he did was catch her on a supposed chance encounter while she was coming down the stairs and he walked up to her and reminded her how they had met at a party, and asked her if she remembered him. Of course, she didn't remember him because they had never met. And she told him so, but he persisted and tried to remind her of a conversation that they never had. And she was still not remembering, but she did think that it was an original way to get to know her. As I said, he was not her type. She was looking for seasoned leather, authentic and aged; he was freshly sawn lumber, green and straight cut. But the thing that caught her attention was his accent. It wasn't something from around there, and that spark in his voice provided the necessary mystery and intrigue to keep the encounter going.

This whole thing with Justine ran hot and cold for years – even after he moved to Philadelphia. They communicated but nothing serious ever ignited; it was always touch and go. The interest never really died, but it never really reached critical mass.

Some of the deepest insights we get of Musk comes from Justine who eventually married Musk and together they had five children – twins and triplets. But that wasn't after almost a decade of this on-and-off courtship.

But that aside, Justine constantly recollects, till today, the way that Musk treated her and how he was as interested in her intelligence as much as he was interested in her physicality. In the beginning, he was persistent, but he didn't smother her. There was this swinging pendulum in how he pursued her. As he turned up the charm, he would also give her room to breathe and give her space to grow. Girls in college aren't looking to get married, and neither was she at that point – there was a lot of things he needed to accomplish, but he did see her in a few different ways. There was no doubt about her being his conquest – it was something he wanted to win. It was something he wanted to possess – and by 'it' I am not referring to Justine, but rather the relationship and the conquest.

Those who know him closely, seem to believe that Musk has the ability to read minds or at least has exhibited numerous instances of extrasensory perception. This is not uncommon for people who have high empathic activity and intelligence. In one display of this ability, Justine talks about the time that Musk called her at a moment in her life when she had decided that, if Musk were to try again in pursuing her, she would relent. Within days of that decision, Musk called and, from that point on, the two became an item – officially.

From the time that he pursued her in Queen's, the friendship had been on and off. She had other intentions, but she was intrigued by him, yet not enough to actually spark the chemistry she saw as the prerequisite for a full-blown relationship.

This went on for years. It started the second year Musk was attending Queen's, and it went on to the point when he had left Penn and moved to California. All this time, there was no relationship but friendship. They spoke often, and they even dated other people. Not only was Justine interested in other men at the time she completed her Journalism degree at Queen's, but Musk was also dating various other women while he was at Queen's during his Sophomore year and on to Penn. He was also dating other women at the time he moved out West.

Even though they were separated by a few hundred miles at first when he was in Philadelphia, he would continuously send her roses. That gesture kept him vivid in her memory so, even if he was out of sight, he certainly wasn't going to allow his presence to be out of mind.

But until they got married, or at least until they started to get on the same page about spending life together, she had swung like a pendulum from love to conquest and back again, numerous times, for him. For her, the relationship was different. Each time was a build-up. Slow like the building of a fire in a castle's hearth. It took her close to a decade before she got to the point that Musk became her soul mate. It took him a look across the common room to decide that she should and would make a good trophy.

The one thing that is clear from the actions Musk took across from the time that they met, the time they dated, the time they remained as friends, the time they were engaged, the time they were married and her time after the messy divorce is that his intentions were always clear – he wanted someone to fit the role he had structured in his mind. Justine happened to be the one that came close and so he took what he could and then tried to cosmetically alter the rest.

Take, for instance, the thing with her hair and hair color. He wanted her to color her hair blonde and she was not a blonde but a pretty brunette. She obliged – this was the first phase of the objectification of Justine. As the years passed, his desire for her to be more blonde became more prevalent. She obliged with each additional tint. How she looked, what she wore, and even what she said was subject to Musk's choreography.

After graduating Queen's, Justine left for Japan while Musk wrapped up his second degree at Penn and then spent some time brainstorming with brother Kimball. He had originally been accepted into the Stanford doctoral program – got there and attended it for a few days and decided that it was not where he wanted to be. He and his younger brother set about getting their heads together on a project that could get them to make money with what they knew how to do. All this time, Justine and Musk continued to communicate, but the flowers stopped while she was out East.

Justine had constantly thought of Musk in her time away, but she hadn't fully reached the place she needed to be. Justine, you see, was and till today remains a die-hard romantic and, as many dates that she may go on, she has always needed to feel her man and she was not there yet.

By the time she got back, Musk was accelerating in his endeavors. In his mind, success was fait accompli; in her mind, the future was uncertain. Not knowing what to do next, she started bartending. Back in Canada, she started to think of Musk even more, and she came to the conclusion that she had missed her opportunity at happiness. Absence certainly does make the heart grow fonder. Her instincts of Musk and him not being the right one for her had faded into the background and what remained in the foreground was her loneliness and the yearning for the attention that he knew how to dole out in abundance. That's when he called, out of the blue, and she stayed true to her utterance. They got together.

By the time she got down to California, Musk was living in a loft with a couple of people and plugging away at his endeavor of Zip2. Zip2 was the online directory that he set up together with his younger brother. When he left Stanford, he shot straight up to Canada and hung out with his brother while they brainstormed an idea to move on. What resulted was Zip2. Remember this was the early 90s and anything you developed that could reside online and provide a service was probably going to make a bit of money.

So, when Justine got to California, Musk was plugging away at Zip2 and trying to make it work. It took some time, but she watched him in his new element, a far cry and a long distance in space and time from the boy that relentlessly pursued her against her polite wishes to the contrary.

They got reacquainted at this time across a number of trips that Justine made, shuttling back and forth between Canada and San Francisco. The conversation didn't rest on platitudes for long and they jumped straight into talk about marriage and kids. Both were on board and they gave themselves two years to put their lives on track. As this happened, Zip2 became a hit and, overnight, Musk went from budding entrepreneur with promise to a multimillionaire. It was a culture shock that Justine had no idea what to do with. Soon, the rented loft turned into a purchased apartment, and the meager transportation they used turned into a McLaren.

Then it was off to the next endeavor, and X.com was born. It was the precursor to PayPal, and this is around the time things started to get a little strange. Aside from the McLaren, the condo, and a couple of small things, most of the money he made from the sale of Zip2 was reinvested into X.com. By November of 1999, just two months before the wedding, Musk had lined up legal representation to put together an agreement that looked, read, and sounded like a prenup, but wasn't a prenup. It wasn't a prenup because Musk said it wasn't. As uncomfortable as Justine was on hearing that the appointment was already set and she just had to show up, she brushed it off as something that Musk was capable of and something that didn't mean that his heart wasn't as far along the spectrum of 'soulmateness.' She let it pass and acquiesced into signing on the dotted line.

Just so we are clear – there was no prior discussion and there was no separate attorney present. There was no heads-up or explanation – just an assurance that it wasn't a prenup and that she had nothing to worry about.

He apparently told her that it wasn't his idea but the requirement by the board of PayPal that was requiring that he did this. That made even less sense to her, but she did not have the slightest inclination to not trust him or not take him at his word. Of course, now when she looks back she feels that none of that was genuine. Whether it was or it wasn't is not up to us to determine or judge. But I specifically include it here to show you the lengths to which an accomplished person would and should go to achieve what he has to achieve. By that, I don't mean that he needs to be okay with sneaking in a prenup (a rose by any other name smells just as sweet) but rather that he sees it as just part and parcel of doing what he needs to do.

Once they signed the document and the wedding went on as scheduled two months later, they settled in to being married after a couple of years of being engaged and almost a decade of being friends. You could say that she knew Musk really well but, at the same time, she was witnessing the metamorphosis of the man we now know as Rocket Man.

As X.com morphed into PayPal and Musk was rolling full steam ahead with it, the lifestyle that was already significantly different from the early days in San Francisco, took another leap. With that leap came direction and the choreography of how Justine was to behave. It was around this time that Alexander was born and this was probably one of the saddest times in all of Musk's existence.

He may not be there for his girlfriends or his wife, but he adores his kids and, when Nevada Alexander was born, Musk was elated and had a very specific framework of how he wanted to raise his son. He didn't have time so he passed that on to Justine, but he was bound and determined to run a tight ship when it came to the raising of his offspring.

The relationship began to show signs of strain that were there all along but were masked by the lifestyle and the excuses of a high-paced career. Justine had to relax the book writing, which had been going well until then and she had already been published. Musk was too focused on his achievements to notice that she was thirsting for her own achievements in the literary world – a world he had proclaimed to understand in word but not in deed, as it turns out.

When Nevada went to sleep one day in his tenth week, he stopped breathing and, by the time the paramedics were alerted and showed up, they were not able to resuscitate him in time to prevent brain damage, and a host of other complications came to pass. The Musks decided to pull the plug after a couple of days on life support, and Justine held baby Nevada in her arms as he slipped away peacefully.

That was traumatic for both of them on so many levels, but it was also the wedge that cracked the stone. That event showed the distinct way the Musks handled their grief. Justine needed someone to talk it through since she was balancing between her post-partum condition and the loss of her first son. But Musk grieved in a different way. He chose to not talk about it – any of it. And so they never did.

Any attempt by Justine to find reprieve was met by Musk's wrath, which was undoubtedly the consequence of his pain.

The solution, he decided, was to get pregnant again without delay so that they could divert their attention to the pregnancy, and later, to the kids that came along. Rather than leave this to chance, Musk insisted that he choreograph this phase of their life as well and they did that by attempting IVF so that the pregnancy could be better timed and better predicted. Their first attempt resulted in twins – two boys.

Prior to the wedding, when the couple was in their happy courting phase, the subject of children had revealed that both Musk and Justine were the kind of people who loved kids and wanted to have at least two or four kids. The difference being predicated on whether there was a nanny to help with the chores. As far as Justine was concerned, she had no idea of the life that Musk had laid out for himself, in the same way an army general lays out his uniform the night before reporting for duty. In his mind, of course, there were going to be nannies and helpers at home.

After the wedding, they had five helpers around the house, so the twin boys were still short of the mark. They went back in for IVF and this time they were blessed with triplets.

Justine's career as a writer came to a halt, and that is to be expected. Parents often sacrifice their dreams to provide for their kids – not just the provision of money and resources, but also the provision of time and love. Justine stepped up admirably and the days of Nevada were in the rear mirror and fading fast.

But something else was in that rear mirror as well and this was not fading, but actually racing up to Justine from behind. As time passed, and X.com became PayPal, and PayPal got purchased by eBay, Musk's wealth had suddenly jumped from the days after Zip2, and now there was some serious money involved. eBay purchased PayPal for a deal valued at $1.5 billion. Musk's take from that was a very cool $165 million. The PayPal transaction closed the week Nevada went to sleep and didn't wake up.

The sudden wealth placed a huge disparity in the marriage. In dollar terms, Justine had contributed nothing. Musk had contributed everything. But in the Calculus of modern man's minds, the contribution women place by raising the family never balances the scales where the man brings in the bacon. That's an unfortunate reality of today's dynamic. It shouldn't be, but it is. And this played out to such obvious levels in the Musk Beverly Hills household. It wasn't just in her head, in fact, he told her, point blank, that he was the Alpha in the relationship.

He handled Nevada's death and his sale of PayPal by throwing himself into the next big thing. He could not fathom why Justine wanted to talk about the past and Justine couldn't figure out why he wanted to silence it. Neither understood each other, but both had valid reasons for what they were doing and how they were feeling.

The battle between the two continued to simmer and smolder in the background – off the main stage that was meticulously choreographed. They would still attend high-dollar functions, still be seen in public, and still move in the right circles. Tesla and Space X had started up and, while things initially went well, the companies started to face trouble and that's when things got even worse at home.

Musk was being tight with cash that he no longer had, falling into debt to make payroll, and he was losing sleep and sanity. Justine had now seen the man she married come full circle. There is only one story sadder than the man who has nothing – that is the man who makes it in every way, then loses it all. Suddenly his alpha was sucked out from under him and he couldn't keep it together, and neither could Justine.

They started seeing a therapist and, after two and a half months of that, he finally couldn't take it and, in his exacting way, sought to place a deadline on the revitalization of the marriage. His deadline was that, if they couldn't make it by the end of the day, they would get divorced in the morning.

The next day, his lawyers prepared the paperwork and he presented it to her along with reference to the 'non-prenup' prenup.

Chapter 9 Life as a Man

"It's pretty hard to get to another star system. Alpha Centauri is four light years away, so if you go at 10 percent of the speed of light, it's going to take you 40 years, and that's assuming you can instantly reach that speed, which isn't going to be the case. You have to accelerate. You have to build up to 20 or 30 percent and then slow down, assuming you want to stay at Alpha Centauri and not go zipping past. It's just hard. With current lifespans, you need generational ships. You need antimatter drives because that's the most mass-efficient. It's doable, but it's super slow."

— Elon Musk

It's easy to find fault with a man's decisions. It is even easy to mock, ridicule, and reign superior in fake morality over a man and the decisions he makes. As much as a man is about the decisions he makes, those decisions do not form in a vacuum due to some magical string of character. It is all formed by the way he treads through the experiences of life. My purpose with looking into the depths of Musk's life and experiences is to learn. Not just from the things he did right, but to learn from the mistakes he made and the errors he didn't see happen. He is not perfect, and I don't expect him to be.

Within the span of eleven years, Musk went from being a high school senior, to arriving in a new country and working odd jobs, enrolling in school, transferring to a new school in a new country, and excelling in areas that he loved and accelerating in deliverable accomplishments. Within 11 years of leaving South Africa and within eight years of coming to America he made his first million (twenty million, actually). What does that say about the art of achievement? What does that say about the path one needs to walk to succeed?

It has been widely reported that Musk has no interest in taking his kids back to Pretoria and have them meet his dad. That's a significant issue for anyone and not one that we should discard in our effort to understand the man that has been hailed as this generation's Edison.

People do certain things because it gives them pleasure, either in the act itself or in the execution of the habit that encompasses it. People typically stay away from things either because they know, at a cerebral level, that the consequences of the act will not be acceptable to the refrain from acts due to a visceral response to the pain that the act causes just by thinking of it.

I have an aversion to alcohol, not because I have some sort of moral guideline, but because at some point the aftereffects of a drink, no matter how small, became intolerably unpleasant. It turns out my constitution couldn't handle it and my body promptly rejected it and, in the process of doing so, made me feel horrible. After repeated experiences of the after effects, my response to anything alcohol was subconsciously dictated by the unpleasantness. I didn't consciously think of it; I just reacted with grimace. My response was not calculated; it was automatic, visceral and visible. What wasn't visible was the memory of the pain that caused the response. All our actions can be measured in similar frameworks. We do everything based on a quantifiable reason even if we don't really know what that is or how it came about.

The point is that sometimes we react to things because of the accumulated unpleasantness that we are subjected to. It is the same way with Musk. The abuse (psychological) was just unbearable to the point that, when the fuse blew, there was no going back. But that sort of thing is not something to judge. The abuse was physical in school and psychological at home. That was just the beginning – then there was the emotional abuse that was a function of the divorce. As the oldest child in the family, there is always a sense of blame that they place on themselves. Whichever way you cut it, the burden that Musk, in his youth, carried was tremendous, and it had a bearing on the man he became.

Fortunately, for us, we can learn from that. The key is to understand who we are and how to keep it together. The thought that Musk is trying to keep it together can be seen in many of the things he says and does. At the end of a conversation with one of his biographers, Musk asks him if he sounds crazy. And that is not the only time; it happens quite a bit. There is the sense of insecurity that pulls on the stings of Musk's frame of mind.

Within a couple of weeks of the divorce from Justine, Musk was back in the saddle again and dating.

Musk has a vision in his head, and that is the point of this chapter and the other chapters that cover his personal life with partners. He has a vision that he is in a race to perfect and make real. He sees in his head that he needs to have a family, a number of kids, a sports car, a certain caliber of friends, a specific type of plane, and certain kinds of names for himself. He has all this in his head, and the way it works is that he just starts gunning for it at a clip that is not typically known to regular people. It may make him seem cold and calculating, but it really isn't. Justine was just another piece of that puzzle that he had to assemble and, when it fell through, he put it in his mental calendar that he needed to fill that void in the overall picture. It was not an emotional investment that most of us make; it was a puncture that most of us don't see.

Is this a good or a bad thing? It's neither. It's just the way he does things. But there is a lesson to be learned. When you go after success, there is no emotional and visceral fantasy – there is just the inspiration to do it and then the march to get it done. It is the surest way to get to where you are going.

Think about marching from New York to Los Angeles. If you were to ever contemplate such a feat, all you would need to do is plan the trip and follow the plan meticulously, without giving up in the event that something outside your plan happened. You would spend as little time as possible correcting your course in the event of a deviation and then get back to it. Plugging away till you get to where you are going.

Most people can't do that. They get distracted. They get blinded. Something else happens that gives them a new goal to shoot for. All sorts of things happen and, in the end, you realize that you are about to retire and none – absolutely none of your dreams have materialized. People like Musk don't have that problem. They coldly calculate where they are going and they march toward its accomplishment relentlessly. Sometimes people around them get hurt, but that, in the minds of people like Musk, is just acceptable collateral damage.

Life as a man is hard enough as it is. And that statement is not about gender equality but about the resources that are backed into us and the way we are raised with expectations. We are like wine, how we are raised – the soil beneath us, the humidity around us, the sun above us, all determine the unique flavor that we begin to mature with. If we change that soil, alter the humidity, or shade the vines from the light, then the taste of the wine thirty years down the road is something very different.

The events that unfolded over the course of Musk's life may not be palpable to some, or may not seem significant to others, but either way, he should not be judged. Musk is neither the Technological Edison of our time nor is he a monster in disguise. He is who he is, and his actions, his mistakes, and his accomplishments have much to teach us. And that is the point of a biography.

There are two things that I have personally learned from Musk's life story as I spent the better part of a year researching the stories and understanding the background. The first is that dream and inspirations, whether they come from within us or from within the pages of a comic, can eventually come true if we put our minds to them. Musk and I share the same generation – that means we share the same comics, the same cartoons, and the same science fiction. We also share the same collective imagination where cartoons like Flash Gordon, Carl Sagan's Cosmos, The Apollo Landing, The Jetsons, Logan's Run and all those TV programs, books, and stories inundated us with ideas of what the future could be. Whether we like it or hate, it, whether we realize it or are oblivious to it, it soaked into our roots, nourished us, and illuminated our minds. Musk grew up to embody that inspiration and you can see it in the projects that he takes – space travel, vacuum tube transportation, electric self-driving vehicles, brain-controlled computers. All the projects he has undertaken are strangely familiar to those of us who share the generational space with Musk. It's what we watched on TV. He just set himself on a path to make it come true.

When it came to relationships, however, there were a few elements at play. The perfect woman had to be in the image of his perfect mother. She was a huge influence in his life and also a source of guilt when he had to move to his father's home because he wanted a man's guiding hand. The South African chauvinist tendencies were not lost on young Musk – and they are still not lost today. Justine thinks that the Alpha in him, which he reminded her of so often, was because he made more than she did, but the truth is that it's not about that entirely, it was also about the fact that the bully-macho South African strain was so deeply rooted in him.

The second was that Musk grew up in a world that was isolated. Whether he was being lectured at by his father in terms that were harsh, or he was hiding from getting beaten in school, or the fact that he hardly had friends of the opposite sex in high school, it caused him to withdraw into his own mental space. Compound that with the fact that he had a unique mental framework that would be able to focus deeply on just about anything he was able to extricate himself from the world around him. It made him a genius, but it also resulted in a very lonely life. That feeling of being lonely was unpleasant and disturbing to him, so he placed that on a list that he was to remedy when he unshackled himself of the chains of his formative years. He cannot stand to be alone and, now that he has the wherewithal, he makes it a point that being alone is not an option.

That is a powerful admission from a man who seems to be able to accomplish anything, and it is one that more of us need to be able to admit to when we feel the need. Most men, and to a large extent women, do not like the idea of being alone but we never get down to realizing it or admitting it to ourselves. Being alone is a scary thought, and it is one that drives us to do a lot of good things, but it is also one that drives us to do a lot of crazy things.

Not wanting to be alone and the fear of sleeping alone at night or not hearing another person's breathing sounds next to you is something that makes absolute sense for a man, and Musk was quickly in the arms of another person as soon as Justine had moved out.

Dating Tallulah Riley happened quick and happened fast, and it seemed like Musk was just heartless. It's not that, and it's not that he didn't love or have real feelings for Justine. It's more that he never wanted to be alone. Even when he split from Riley, he jumped into the arms of someone else and just kept looking for that perfect partner.

It is not that he is a bad person, it is that he is driven by fear and it shows in many of the things he says and does. We are all the same way, but we can learn to be stronger by learning from the people that we read about. But just because Musk has certain weaknesses doesn't mean that the lessons he can teach us to achieve amazing things should be discarded.

Musk is a man of tremendous talent and work ethic. He does not take his gifts for granted, and he does not waste them. He may be someone that lacks original ideas, but he is a man that takes ideas that are on the shelf and makes them work.

Chapter 10 The Future According to Musk

"No, I don't ever give up. I'd have to be dead or completely incapacitated."

— Elon Musk

We've spent much of the book looking at the shadow of the man's mind to be able to get an idea of the share of his real being. That's the best way to go about understanding a person and his motivations. Everything we do has a wave that ripples away from that and, if we can't see the event hidden underwater, we can certainly observe the tsunami it creates on the surface.

That's what this biography has been repeatedly doing.

Looking at his words and deeds gives us a credible way of piecing together his motivations and the projection of his thoughts.

If there is one thing that you cannot disagree with, it is that Musk has a vivid imagination. Even if this was fired up by all the comics he read and TV he watched. Don't mock it because some of the greatest ideas and inventions came from fiction writers like Isaac Asimov. As an integrated society coming ever closer to each other with the prevalence of technology, Musk sits at the juxtaposition of two worlds. A world where his imagination was stirred by the greatest dreamers of our time when we were kids, and he brings that along and converts it into our reality. I for one am grateful that all the things I saw as a kid on TV are getting built in reality in my generation. And we have Musk to thank for that.

The other side of the equation is that Musk's own imagination is now poised to field the imagination of the generation that is sitting in front of their TV (or iPhone) watching the launch of the Falcon Heavy and, as those rockets ignite, so do the minds of millions of kids around the world. Hats off to someone like Musk for doing that. We would not have been able to if there wasn't someone like Musk who could take whatever had happened in his life and then keep moving. We needed someone to not be distracted by the everyday distractions that cross our path every hour, every minute and, sometimes every second.

He started young and at the age of 12 wrote and sold his first computer game for $500. I am not going to try to put that into perspective but, just to say that, if you remove the quantum of the payoff and the fact that he was twelve, you are left with the fact that Musk was in this game when computers were just starting to make it into the mainstream. It was 1984 and not everybody knew what computers did or how to use them, and this person got over all that and made some money accomplishing something in a new industry. That's an accomplishment for anyone at any age.

Then he went on to run a number of small businesses in the dorms by making and upgrading computers and game boxes – not much of a big deal there but still, most of the kids I knew in college just went to school and spent their time hanging out.

Then came the time that he was making money on campus at Penn by doing parties and charging a five-buck cover. He and his partner made enough in one night to cover rent for a month. Calling it enterprising doesn't seem to cover it.

Then came the big ideas. He came out and did Zip2 while he was at Stamford – which he left after a short while then roped his brother into the software ideas he was working on. If you haven't Googled it already, Zip2 is a kind of a directory that visualizes the advertiser on a map. It is something like what Google Maps does. It's just that this was a year ahead of Google. Google started their search business in 1998 and didn't bring on their Google Maps till much later. But the idea of Google Maps was pretty much something that resembled Zip2.

His next idea was X.com, and we know that became PayPal, and we know how that ended and then that gave rise to Space X and Tesla. These companies, as much as they are a hit today, had their share of teething pains when they first started. The headaches that they caused were no small matter. It affected Musk at a deep and psychological level, and he just couldn't bring himself to accept defeat. But before that, he had already started investing in other endeavors. While he was at the tail end of PayPal, he invested in a company that was founded by his childhood buddy and cousin, Lyndon Rive. That company, Everdream Corp, sold to Dell and Musk made some profit from that sale.

In the same fashion, he invested in a satellite company while he was in the midst of building Space X. The synergy was obvious and he wanted to make sure that he also had a client in the area that would one day be able to use Space X's services. He was made a director of the company, which he eventually left to focus on his other more urgent businesses.

He then invested and promoted Solar X, which is still ongoing and looks to revolutionize the way we harvest and distribute energy. He has changed not just the infrastructure and the source of energy, but the architecture of the distributions and consumption of it. This is a holistic reinvention of the way we see and use power.

But his investments and his smaller involvements that we know about splashed on newspapers and online are not the extent of his entrepreneurial endeavors. There are more to come and, with the well-known endeavors as a backdrop and the new endeavors as a guide; you start to see where he wants to take the world.

Space X itself is seen as a rocket company. But don't get confused with the blast offs and the launch of the Roadster into space. I admit my experience with the live telecast distracted me away from the true jewel that this is. While most of the hardware is off the shelf, and the additional hardware that went on top of it was purpose-built, the software coordinating the whole thing and the software running the individual systems was built from scratch.

He has, of course, mooted the Hyperloop and he has taken positions with PayPal's competitor, Stripe. He has also made a number of investments in AI companies and, according to him, the investment is not for profit sake but rather to keep an eye on the progress of AI. There is something about AI that really spooks Musk, and he has been warning everyone around him that AI is the doom of the world. That is not unexpected really because, if you've been paying attention, the way it has developed has been on the back of TV programs and movies. When you look at the way movies have viewed AI and the takeover of the world, you can imagine what's fueling his imagination.

That brings me to the bulk of his drive and passion.

The future according to Musk, is really the future that luminaries like Carl Sagan and Isaac Asimov have imagined. This avid reader has taken the imagination of those men and made something of it. So, let's give credit where credit is due.

While Musk is not the visionary that everyone thinks he is, he certainly has the drive to make things happen. We need all kinds in this world. Think about the atom bomb, for instance. It was based on Einstein's equation – the idea and the theory – but the bomb itself was built by a different group of people. Think about Apple. The computer itself was built by Woz, but Jobs was the one that pushed it to success. There are many kinds of success and, if we really want to find the string that vibrates in each, then we have to speak the truth of what it is that makes them succeed. If you are a fan of Musk, but you are looking for that original idea, then you are in the wrong shoes.

The best thing that you can take from Musk's experience depends on two things. The first depends on your own personal situation, and the second is the way you choose to see the accomplishments Musk has made in the course of the last twenty years, and beyond.

Musk is undoubtedly a complex character. And I urge you to not fault his weakness but to spend your energy understanding them so that you can sidestep those same mistakes.

Soon after his payday from the Zip2 deal, aside from the F1 that he purchased, he also bought a single-engine aircraft, no doubt prompted by the ghosts of his memories and imagination kindled by the stories of Grandpa Haldeman.

It took him close to six months to get the license, and that's not because getting a single-engine Airplane Private Pilot's license is the hardest thing in the world, but because he had to spend time doing so many things in the wake of the Zip2 transaction.

But his enthusiasm to fly is not one that is in passing. He does see himself being able to pilot the vehicle to Mars one day and he does see himself dying on Mars sometime in the future – just not at the same time.

The vision for Mars that he has is one that is not only deeply-seated, but one that comes naturally to him. There are certain things that you come across in life that you just know you will do or accomplish. There are certain things I know with such certainty in my life that I don't worry about whether it is going to happen; I just get impatient that today was not the day that it happened. Musk is the same way

– we are all for a different number of things. For Bill Clinton, he knew on the day he shook JFK's hand that he would one day be President. For Einstein, he knew one day he would build a life around a world deciphering the secrets of the Universe, unlike his father's direction to be an engineer and to make a living. For Edison, he knew that the light bulb, and so many other inventions, were just a matter of time. In the same way, Musk knows with certainty that walking on Mars is in his future and, because of that, we can also know with confidence that our species landing on Mars is in our future as well.

That is the real value of Musk in our society; he raises all up to a point that we can only imagine. His dreams are the dreams of a nation, of a planet, and of this species. I know, sitting and watching the launch of Falcon Heavy, that it dawned on me that I had been waiting for this moment for such a long time – in fact, I had given up on it because no one was doing it. Sure, there was talk of it from Branson's Virgin Galactic. Sure, there was talk from Bezos's Blue Origin, but that was all talk, conjecture, and trials. This was real.

Watching Falcon Heavy blast into space with such apparent ease, experiencing the exhilaration of the people on the ground as the mighty rocket lifted effortlessly into space and released its payload was just a childish sense of excitement that I have not felt since my dad took us to the screening of the first Star Wars installment.

Musk made all that come to life. And for that I am grateful.

There is much we can learn for the life that Musk has led. There is much that we can observe in the decisions and in the mistakes he has made. The one that is most obvious is that anybody can be whatever they dream of as long as they are willing to never give up.

Conclusion

"I would like to die on Mars. Just not on impact."

— Elon Musk

There is a long list of men and women who have risen to the surface of the world's collective consciousness and appreciation. In the generation before mine, it was people like JP Morgan, Thomas Edison, Marie Curie, and Albert Einstein. In this generation, the pinnacle is populated by the likes of Bill Gates, Steve Jobs, Stephen Hawking, and Elon Musk.

I find tremendous inspiration looking at the men in this generation that have moved mountains aside and brought planets closer. I have looked at the lives and accomplishments of men like Sir Richard Branson, Steve Jobs, Bill Gates, and a number of others and find that all these men have similar DNA when it comes to key areas. The most common of all is that these men are unrelenting in their pursuit and unyielding in the realization of their dream.

Musk is at the top of that list. He came to North American shores with a dream and a couple of hundred dollars, with no one that he could rely on and no one he could spend the night with. He pushed his way out of a repressive society under a racist regime and focused on the area that best suited what he wanted to do, then did not give up. How many of us can say they pursued their dreams across the horizon? How many of us can say that we never took no for an answer?

To the common eye, Musk is obsessive in his pursuit. For anyone to be successful, that is a prerequisite. Jobs was the same way. Musk, however, has labored to portray his life in a manner that is choreographed and precise. It follows from a choreography that started with his relationships, his aspirations, the resulting achievements, and the lifestyle. All of it is highly planned and executed, and the ones that don't fit in are altered or enhanced. Like Justine's and Tallulah's hair color.

You wouldn't think it, but Musk is indeed a master of illusions. He is a genius at making things happen, but then there are the details of his imagination that, when they do not appear, causes him to go through the trouble of airbrushing when he can. But I have to give him a lot of credit for that because this is a man that sees an image in his head and is relentless at seeing it get done. He's like Arnold Schwarzenegger in that way. Schwarzenegger had a vision of what his body should look like back in the day when he was a bodybuilder and he would relentlessly pursue it regardless of how much it hurt or whatever the pain entailed.

Musk did the same thing. He didn't just get into that furnace – in what must have felt like the depths of hell – and work at it, but he had a vision that he was working toward and he pulled it off.

The loyalty to the image you have in your head is what makes a man accomplish what he needs to accomplish. That is the first rule, ahead of all rules. Anything less renders the vision as a fantasy and nothing more.

Musk took a huge risk in moving himself from Pretoria to Canada; he took a huge risk in traveling across the country looking for relatives, and he took huge risks in investing in space and automobile technologies.

But risk to a man in that space is not the same as the risk to a man that is not bound for success. The path to success is not carved by the knife of chance; it is paved by the lessons of mistakes.

Most of you see risk as something to mitigate. By looking at risk as inevitable, you see the inevitability of failure. For those who succeed, be it Jobs or Musk, Gates or Jack Ma, success is inevitable. The risk they take is not the risk you fathom. To them, it is just a path that can be overcome with relentless effort and a keen mind for observation. You don't need to be extra smart or have an IQ of 180. You must be willing to learn and willing to make mistakes and pull yourself back up.

Musk is not someone who has had success after success and not tasted failure. That is furthest from the truth. There have been times that he has made mistakes and there are times that he failed. Take the company that he invested in and was quite gung-ho about. It was a company that was trying to perfect human genome sequencing. It was a company where you'd walk up to them, give them a sample of your blood, wait ten minutes and they would give you a detailed readout of your genetic sequence. Sounds simple enough but Musk couldn't make it work and, with the times he knows that it is not about the effort, he knows when to fold.

'To thine own self be true,' says the master of literature, William Shakespeare. I find that whatever his characteristics and whatever his flaws the one thing that Musk has always been clear about, regardless of what words he uses to express it, is that he has always been true to himself. He understands his needs, his dreams, and he understands the resources that he has within him to make the leap from not having something to make it materialize.

All his decisions were made along these principles and he knew how to be true to himself. It's just one less distraction to deal with when you know that you want to see your rocket take flight, but you don't have the design to do it. Instead of forcing something to work that doesn't, he found the path to making it a reality by besting the old designs. Putting together the Falcon and Dragon designs based on existing hardware but cutting down on areas that were unnecessary and supplementing it with software, made the rockets lift more into space for less, in terms of resources and propellant. It may be a large carbon footprint, but his computations and design ideas made that footprint 70% less than what it would have been for the same payload.

Musk isn't this generation's Edison, just as Einstein wasn't the last generation's Newton. They were two different men thrust into two different times, with two different environments who accomplished two very different accomplishments. We have proven that we couldn't do without Edison's creations, just as history will prove in a few hundred years that we wouldn't have made it without Musk's current efforts. His fear that we are running out of time in terms of the environmental degradation will work to humanity's eventual benefit. If it wasn't for his fears that the rest of us seem so oblivious to, we might just be faced with not having the necessary lifeline that gives our species a way to extend our existence without perishing under the burden of a rapidly changing environment. His notion to terraform Mars and to create a viable means to transport society there will be the lifeline we need in times to come.

I wish him Godspeed!

If you enjoyed learning about Elon Musk, I would be forever grateful if you could leave a review on Amazon. Reviews are the best way to help your fellow readers find the great books so make sure to help them out! Thanks in advance!

Make sure to check out the first book in this 'Billionaire Visionaries' series:

Jeff Bezos: The Force Behind the Brand

Printed in Great Britain
by Amazon

36087918R00078